Empowering
Children & Young People

Empowering
Children & Young People

Promoting involvement in decision-making

Lina Fajerman and Phil Treseder

Save the Children

About the author

As a young person, Phil Treseder was involved with a wide variety of projects including the International Year of the Child, International Youth Year and the British Youth Council. He went on to work as Development Officer for the Wales Youth Forum, and as an assessor for the European Commission Youth Initiative Project fund. The information contained in this pack is based on Phil Treseder's experiences of working for the Children's Rights Development Unit, and subsequent responsibility for the early development of Article 12. Phil Treseder is currently working freelance.

Acknowledgements

I would like to thank the following people for their help in preparing these guidelines: the staff of the Children's Rights Development Unit, Alison, Miriam and Saskia and in particular Gerison Lansdown and Issy Cole-Hamilton for their help in developing the initial idea; all those who attended the first brainstorming meeting; Dynamix Ltd – Creative Training Agency; Save the Children; Pat Gordon-Smith.

I would like to dedicate these guidelines to all the children and young people with whom I have worked, and particularly to those involved in Article 12, Voices from Care and the Wales Youth Forum. Thanks also to John Collins, the person responsible for getting me into this line of work to begin with, and subsequently failing to to talk me back out of it.

Published by
Save the Children
17 Grove Lane
London SE5 8RD

Registered charity no: 213890

First published 1997
Reprinted 2004

© Save the Children and the Children's Rights Office 1997

All rights reserved. No reproduction, copy or transmission of this publication may be made without written permission, except under the terms below.

This publication is copyright, but may be reproduced by any method without fee or prior permission for teaching purposes, but not for resale. For copying in any other circumstances prior written permission must be obtained from the publisher and a fee may be payable.

ISBN 1 899120 47 5

Edited by Pat Gordon Smith
Designed by Micheline Mannion
Typeset by Nancy White
Printed by Page Brothers

Contents

Foreword by Article 12   2

Introduction   3

Part 1 Professional development

  1 Moving towards empowerment   6
     Exercises 1–2   9–10

  2 The benefits of empowerment   11
     Exercises 3–5   15–21

  3 Tackling the barriers to empowerment   22
     Exercises 6–9   31–5

Part 2 Working with children and young people

  4 Preparing children and young people for involvement   38
     Exercises 10–14   48–52

  5 Initial involvement   55
     Exercises 15–17   61–5

Part 3 Long-term involvement

  6 Developing policy and practice   68

  7 Examples of good practice   75

Bibliography and further reading   95

Foreword

This is not the theory of empowerment. This is not someone writing about something they do not know. This is not merely a book about the latest buzz-word. This is a guide to empowering children and young people.

As members of Article 12 we've had the pleasure of working with Phil for two years. In that time, we've come to respect him and the other members of Article 12. Empowerment is a long word with, no doubt, many definitions, but if empowerment means giving and sharing, if empowerment means creating respect, if empowerment means equality for all, and if empowerment means taking control of our own lives, then Phil has helped empower us.

Article 12 is an up-and-coming organisation run by young people, for young people. We are named after Article 12 in the UN Convention (see page 3) which states that a child who is capable of forming his or her own views has 'the right to express those views freely, in all matters affecting the child', or, as the unofficial summary puts it, 'the child has a right to express an opinion, and to have that opinion taken into account in any matter of procedure affecting the child'.

Article 12 is made up of young people from all around the country. At the moment we are still small, but with help, and perhaps a bit more cash, we hope to become a national, or even global, voice for children and young people. The difference between us and other organisations is that in Article 12 the power lies in the hands of the young people themselves.

Phil has played a big part in the development of Article 12, as our co-worker, unofficial secretary and all-round dogsbody. Although he has recently left us for greener pastures, he still helps us and his legacy will live on. Without his commitment, Article 12 would not be what it is today. Now read his book…

Anil and Nikhil Gomes (aged 16 and 14), on behalf of Article 12

Introduction

In December 1991, the UK Government ratified the United Nations (UN) Convention on the Rights of the Child. By so doing it made a commitment under international law to comply with the Convention's principles and standards. Perhaps the most significant and far-reaching principle contained in the Convention is Article 12, the right of all children capable of expressing a view to express that view on all matters of concern to them, and to have that view taken seriously. The principle applies to individual decisions affecting a particular child and to matters affecting children as a body. It also extends to decisions made within the family, in schools, and to those providing services as well as to policy-makers and politicians. If fully implemented, this principle would radically change the status and visibility of children within our society. But, to date, it is clear that the opportunity to participate effectively in all the decisions that affect them is not the experience of most children.

During a consultation exercise undertaken in 1993 by the Children's Rights Development Unit, 45 groups of children aged between five and 18 years were approached to discuss their perceptions of how their rights were respected (CRDU 1994). The children came from a wide variety of backgrounds, but common to all groups was a powerful sense of frustration that their views and experiences were not taken seriously at home, at school, by politicians, by policy-makers and by the media. Research into bullying being undertaken at Sheffield University reveals that as many as 50% of children fail to report experiences of bullying because they have no confidence that teachers will listen sufficiently seriously to take action on their behalf (Sharp and Smith 1991). Research into the views of young people in care indicates that effective participation in decision-making processes is not yet a reality for substantial numbers of young people in care. Of 600 young people taking part in a recent survey into the experiences of care, as many as two in five felt that they were not listened to in case conferences and reviews (Who Cares Trust & National Consumer Council 1993). The list of examples is endless. Indeed, when the Committee on the Rights of the Child, the international monitoring body, examined the UK government on its record in implementing the Convention, it specifically criticised the failure to take action to promote Article 12 and recommended that new ways of promoting children's participation should be developed.

The responsibility does not only rest with the government. Everyone working with children and young people needs to explore how to ensure that the principle of listening to children and taking them seriously is integral to their work. There are many exciting new initiatives taking place to create opportunities for promoting participation:

- Birmingham City Council has developed a three-year project with Save the Children to pilot methods of consulting with young people on local policy issues.
- The Guide Association Junior Council members have produced a training document for guiders on the implications of the Convention for their organisation.
- The Association of London Government has agreed to develop a London strategy for adopting the UN Convention and drawing up children's plans.
- Kirklees Metropolitan Borough has developed a children's service plan within the framework of the Convention and identified indicators and targets for its implementation.
- The Royal College of Nursing, with the support of the Gulbenkian Foundation, has initiated annual awards for new developments promoting children's participation in health care services.

However, as yet these are only isolated examples. In most organisations, responsibility for making decisions, as well as involvement in the process, remains firmly in the hands of adults. Changing patterns of decision-making is not easy. There are no blueprints, it is time-consuming, and there is often a lack of clarity about what participation is seeking to achieve. This manual hopes to ensure success by providing professionals with:

- food for *thought* by explaining the benefits of empowerment and defusing the perceived barriers to its introduction;
- real *direction* through examples of good practice and a course of exercises that empower professionals to empower the young people they work with.

Using the manual

Empowering children and young people is addressed to professionals and organisations who work with

children and young people in a range of settings, including residential care workers, community workers, school teachers, local authorities and voluntary organisations. The manual aims to help professionals make empowerment a reality for all children so that they can contribute to the decisions which affect them as individuals and as a group; at unit, local and national levels. In the course of its discussion the manual examines:
- the importance of empowerment to children and young people;
- the benefits of empowerment to children and professionals alike;
- the barriers to empowerment;
- the need for workers and organisations to understand their own intentions before embarking on moves towards empowerment.

The manual's text and exercises combine as a tool for training professionals and young people. Part 1 concentrates on describing participation to professionals, with exercises at the end of each chapter to help professionals work through the issues relating to empowering children and young people in their own working context. Part 2 focuses on training young people to be active in decision-making by building their confidence and understanding of how to be empowered, with end-chapter exercises that are practical ideas for early work with children. Part 3 looks at long-term empowerment, and strategies for making it work are discussed through examples of good practice.

All the material is photo-copyable, and the checklists and exercises in particular have been designed to be photocopied as handouts.

Professionals will need to bear in mind the level of experience of the children they are working with and adapt some of the exercises accordingly. However, it is important to bear in mind that quite young children can display a considerable awareness and maturity when discussing issues which concern them. It is important not to underestimate them.

The text in *Empowering children and young people* is relevant to the empowerment of all children and young people, whatever their age. However, the exercises are aimed at professionals working with children of eight years and above. For those working with younger children, a resource pack entitled *Never too young: How young children can take responsibility and make decisions* is available from the National Early Years Network and Save the Children.

Terms used in the manual

To ensure clarity of meaning, it is helpful to define some key terms which are used in the text and exercises.

The terms **empowerment** and **participation** are central to the discussion. They are to some extent interchangeable, though empowerment is more assertive and implicitly invokes the power relationship. The most constructive means of defining these two terms is to consider participation as the process and empowerment as the outcome.

Involvement is the overall term for children and young people being included in the decision-making process, at any level. The levels of involvement begin with tokenism and end with control.

Consultation is a process which requires the commitment to take on board young people's views and present detailed information back to them. Consultation can be an ongoing process. For instance, a local authority might consult regularly with a permanently established council of young people.

Tokenism is the one-off involvement of children and young people in a decision-making process without follow-up or involvement in the ongoing process. An example of tokenism might be a local authority which requests young peoples' ideas for the design of recreation rooms in an annexe to be built on their residential unit without providing full budget details or real information about the available options, and then refuses to be challenged on the final decision. Children often describe school councils as tokenistic.

Young people have reached a position of **control** when an organisation or project is run by them, with adults acting only in an advisory capacity or having no involvement at all.

In the context of this manual, the word **adult** is used to describe someone who does not use services and who is in a position of control as worker, manager or other professional. In some circumstances the term might also include parents.

An attempt has been made to describe service users as **children and young people**. For ease of language, however, it is not always possible to use the expression in full and so the terms **children** and **young people** used separately should be understood to imply the whole description.

1 Moving towards empowerment

With the right input from management and staff it is possible to involve children in just about any decision that affects them. From developing policies to interviewing staff, inspecting services or educating peers, there need be no limit to children's potential involvement, so long as the process is properly thought out, is appropriate to the environment and suitable resources are available. Unfortunately, many attempts to involve children and young people end in frustration precisely because the implications of empowerment are not properly considered at the start. If an organisation wishes to encourage participation, colleagues must first agree on aims, objectives and expected outcomes, and everyone must understand how far children will be involved in the decision-making process. Failure to establish these fundamentals will almost certainly lead to failure of the overall project.

The questions in **Exercise 1** (page 9) will help professionals consider the issues of empowerment, and can be used to kick off discussions about empowerment and participation in any context. They might initially be thought about by an individual seeking to introduce the concept of empowerment to colleagues, but will also work as a brainstorming session among groups of colleagues. If there is a clear intention to increase children's involvement in decision-making, all professionals should have considered these issues.

Who has control?

Promoting opportunities for children and young people to participate in decisions affecting policies and the delivery of services within an organisation will necessarily have an impact both on the way decisions are made and the nature of those decisions. Most organisations providing services for children do not currently involve users in decisions about the way services are run. Doing so may involve very considerable change in the culture and style of the organisation, and will certainly mean that those who have responsibility for making decisions will need to be prepared to share some of that responsibility. There are a number of questions that will need to be addressed in thinking through how that process can be managed:

- who currently makes what level of decision? If an organisation wishes to create opportunities for children to be involved, it needs to be aware of how decisions are currently made, where power lies within the organisation and what structures exist for making decisions;
- what decisions are the organisation seeking to involve children in? By identifying exactly what it is you are trying to achieve, it will become clearer who you need to involve and at what level in the organisation;
- are you proposing to consult with children in order to better inform your decisions, or are you seeking to establish real opportunities for children to contribute to decision-making? Both approaches are valid as long as you are explicit and honest with children and young people about what you are trying to achieve, but they involve very different methods of involvement. The latter requires a preparedness to share power and will necessitate the active support of those within the organisation who hold access to budgets and who have authority to make the decisions in which you propose to involve children.

Figure 1.1

Degrees of participation

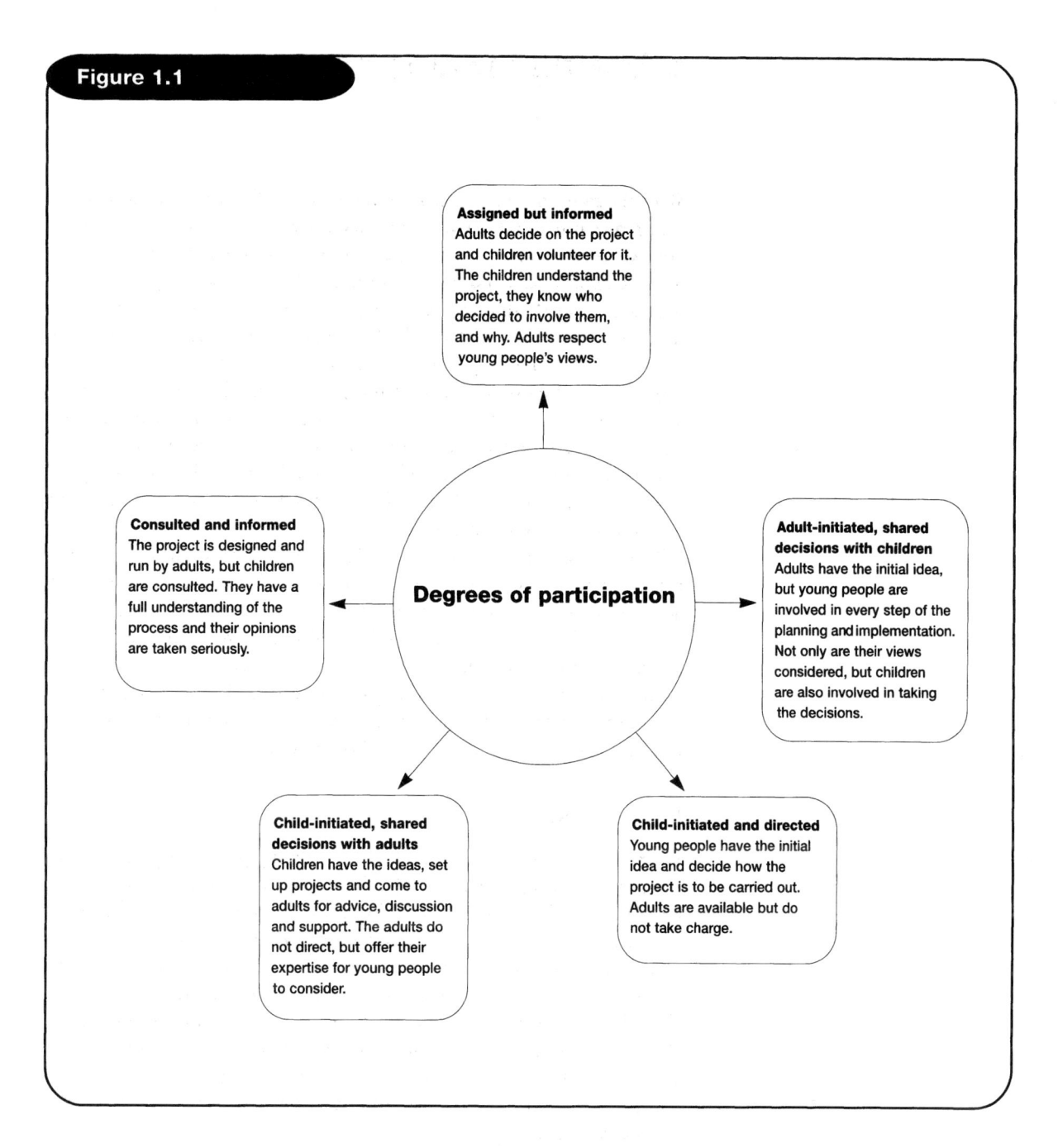

Assigned but informed
Adults decide on the project and children volunteer for it. The children understand the project, they know who decided to involve them, and why. Adults respect young people's views.

Consulted and informed
The project is designed and run by adults, but children are consulted. They have a full understanding of the process and their opinions are taken seriously.

Adult-initiated, shared decisions with children
Adults have the initial idea, but young people are involved in every step of the planning and implementation. Not only are their views considered, but children are also involved in taking the decisions.

Child-initiated, shared decisions with adults
Children have the ideas, set up projects and come to adults for advice, discussion and support. The adults do not direct, but offer their expertise for young people to consider.

Child-initiated and directed
Young people have the initial idea and decide how the project is to be carried out. Adults are available but do not take charge.

The act of consulting children is the first step away from non-participative organisation, but is not an end in itself. Consultation can mean so many things – from eliciting opinion which is managed later, to a hands-off encouragement of self-determination – and so it is crucial that all colleagues work towards an agreed degree of consultation and participation.

Figure 1.1 displays the degrees of participation in a circular layout, but is adapted from the 'Ladder of Participation' which appears in *Child's Participation: From Tokenism to Citizenship* (Hart 1992). This ladder shows participation as a progressive hierarchy, with 'Assigned but Informed' participation on the ladder's bottom rung and 'Child-initiated and Directed' participation sitting at the top. It is an excellent metaphor though, to a certain extent, it limits the choices for those wishing to involve children. The ladder assumes that child-initiated and directed participation is the eventual aim for all those who wish to empower children and young people, and that other 'levels' of participation are merely steps on the way to that eventual goal. This overlooks the fact that child-initiated and directed participation may be inappropriate in some contexts, in which case it could not be seen as an aim of any kind. It is therefore preferable to regard the five degrees of participation as five different, but equal, forms of good practice and to choose the one which will have the most benefit in a specific environment.

Exercise 2 (page 10) is designed to provide a clear representation of who has control in an organisation, though it will also reflect opinions about who has control – some of which may be incorrect, though any such misconceptions will be illuminating in themselves.

Conditions for empowerment

In *Participation of Children and Young People in Social Work* (1995), David Hodgson identifies the need for five conditions which must be met if participation by children and young people is to achieve its goal of empowerment. They are:
- access to those in power;
- access to relevant information;
- genuine choice between distinctive options;
- a trusted independent person who will provide support and, where necessary, be a representative;
- a means of redress for appeal or complaint.

These five conditions cannot be introduced incrementally. They apply in all five degrees of participation which appeared in Figure 1.1 and must be present from the very first involvement of children in decision-making. In some contexts, establishing a framework which satisfies these conditions may be a challenge in itself, but for children and young people to take advantage of participation there must also be some motivation, and, where necessary, training to enable young people to make the best of their powers. Part 2 describes a number of ways in which professionals can help children learn to prioritise and to have confidence in their own opinions.

exercise 1

Key issues

Aim
To identify views about the process and implications of empowerment.

Group size
Individuals (as reflective exercise), small groups or a whole staff

Materials
Pen and paper, or flipchart and marker pens

Consider and write down responses to the following questions, or brainstorm responses if working in a group.

1. What are you aiming to achieve by empowering the children and young people you work with?

2. Where are you in relation to that aim?

3. What will the children and young people get out of it?

4. Are you prepared for the resource implications?

5. Why have you not done it before?

6. Are you prepared to involve children and young people from the start?

7. Are you being honest with the children and young people?

8. What are your expectations?

9. Are you prepared to give up some power?

10. Are you prepared to take some criticism?

11. Do you recognise this as a long-term commitment?

12. Are you prepared to institutionalise the change?

Evaluation:
None. This exercise should involve a free flow of opinions.

Note:
Some of these questions may be difficult to answer at an early stage. All the issues involved are discussed in this manual and it will become easier to pinpoint responses to difficult questions later on. This exercise can be redone as often as required.

exercise 2

The power grid

Aim
To establish where the power lies in an organisation and identify where power could be redistributed to achieve greater involvement for young people.

Group size
Individuals (as reflective exercise), small groups or a whole staff

Materials
Pens and paper, or flipchart and marker pens

1. Brainstorm a list of decisions which are key to the daily, weekly, monthly and annual running of your organisation. For instance, a residential unit may identify the following decisions:
   - setting negotiable rules, e.g. staying-out times, bedtimes, getting-up times, smoking, visiting, privacy, use of kitchen, use of laundry facilities;
   - deciding where to go on holiday;
   - monitoring the budget for holidays and days out;
   - preparing information for other children and young people about the centre;
   - involvement in interviewing and appointing staff.

2. Draw a grid like the one below with the same three headings across the top, entering your list of decisions in the left-hand column.

	Young people have control	Workers have control	Local authority has control
Setting negotiable rules	1	1	3
Deciding where to go on holiday	2	2	1
Involvement in interviewing and appointing staff	3	2	1

3. Enter either 1, 2 or 3 in the corresponding part of the grid to show how much power the young people, workers and local authority have in making any particular decision. You do not have to enter all three numbers. If you think that two groups share the same amount of power, they will share the same number.

4. Discuss the grid's implications and consider where it might be possible to transfer some power to young people in order to increase their participation. This is a good time to think about the part played by your local authority, and whether it will aid or hinder empowerment.

Evaluation:
It will be useful to see if there is a gap between where real control lies, and where individuals perceive it to be. If such a gap exists, the perceptions should be taken as the most telling indicator for where an organisation lies in terms of empowerment.

Note:
This activity can be adapted for young people to work on as part of a consultation exercise.

2 The benefits of empowerment

As we have seen, Article 12 of the UN Convention on the Rights of the Child not only demands that children are entitled to express their views on matters of concern to them, but also that those views are given proper consideration. It is an important principle, but what do children actually get out of it? Tam Tansey of Youth Clubs UK has identified seven clear benefits of empowerment for young people:

1 *A voice and an influence.* Empowerment offers children a level of influence and an element of choice about the kind of provision offered by a service. It helps children and young people be clear about and understand their own wants and needs.
2 *Updated services.* The process of empowerment impels services to meet changing needs that arise from the everyday interests and problems defined by young people.
3 *Child development.* In being empowered, young people experience many new aspects of their own potential, including the dilemma of responsibility and the ability to prioritise.
4 *Social and political education.* Empowerment provides opportunities to acquire the skills of debate, communication, negotiation and individual or group decision-making. In itself, it represents the first steps in learning about how individual, group and even national politics work.
5 *Creators not consumers.* Through empowerment children are encouraged to be active in creating the services they use, rather than being passive consumers of services provided for them. It follows that any such service must be an agent for social change and not one for social control.
6 *Participation in the wider society.* Children with experience of participation in a safe environment will understand the process of empowerment and be better prepared to participate in decision-making when they have moved into wider society.
7 *Democracy.* The promotion and practice of a service which is open and accountable to its users encourages democratic procedures and respect for the principles of democratic life.

To help professionals appreciate the personal benefits of involvement, **Exercise 3** (page 15) asks them to reflect on the meaning of empowerment, and to recognise the occasions when they have personally been empowered. **Exercise 4** (page 20) looks at the double-edged sword of responsibility – its gains *and* losses to young people and organisations.

Good practice

The only meaningful way to investigate the benefits of empowerment is to reflect on occasions where it has worked, particularly where change in practice has profited both young people and adults. The following example of consultation on a Cardiff housing estate produced quantifiable results for all those involved in the exercise. It is useful to bear Tam Tansey's seven points in mind when reading it to see whether, or how, each of them comes into play.

case study

Consulting young people on a Cardiff housing estate

- Issues for young people and community identified through consultation.

At the end of 1989, the National Association for the Care and Resettlement of Offenders (NACRO) led a group of agency representatives in a meeting to discuss their concerns about crime and young people in the Llanedeyrn and Pentwyn areas of their estate. The police were receiving a constant stream of complaints from residents about 'youth annoyance' and the relationship between the police and the estate's young people was very poor. At the meeting of agency representatives, disillusionment was seen to be an indirect reason behind the tendency of some young people to offend and it was agreed that an inter-agency approach was required to improve the situation.

- Further consultation with young people.

Following this meeting, NACRO and the other agencies (which included the Youth Service and Wales Youth Forum) carried out interviews with young people and put together a detailed area profile. From this, they drew up a programme of action which identified several key issues to be addressed, one of which was a recommendation to establish a Youth Forum in Llanedeyrn and Pentwyn. During the consultation exercise, many of the young people questioned had declared a willingness to participate in discussions to plan and implement services. NACRO felt that such participation would help promote a sense of ownership in those services, along with greater responsibility towards the immediate environment and integration with service providers.

- Youth Service seen as most appropriate agency. Main issue of concern to be tackled first.

The Youth Service had been identified as the most appropriate agency to facilitate a Youth Forum on the estate as it was already in contact with a substantial proportion of young people who were indulging in perceived antisocial behaviour. The ultimate aim was to create a representative forum of young people who could be included in many aspects of decision-making, though it was agreed that the forum would only be successful if it:
- dealt first with a single important issue which would lead clearly to practical benefits for young people;
- involved as many young people as possible.

Meetings

- Open invitation to all young people to attend meeting.

An open invitation was issued to all young people living on the estate to attend a meeting. They were informed that the purpose of the meeting was to discuss issues that they perceived as important, and were told which professionals would be at the meeting. These were to be the LEA Youth Worker, a NACRO representative and someone from the Wales Youth Forum.

- Young people agree on issue to be tackled.

This meeting started off with nine young women between the ages of 14 and 17 and they were later joined by 22 other young people, mostly male, of the same age. The young women expressed feelings about police harassment in the area, and these were confirmed and reinforced by the young men, many of whom had been chased by the police that evening. It was felt that this was an issue which affected the young people's day-to-day lives, so harassment became the focus of the forum – the 'single important issue' on which involvement would hopefully reap 'practical benefits' for the young people.

- Problems identified.

Much of the conversation of this first meeting focused on the definition of 'harassment', and it was agreed that this did not include any incident in which an offence was committed. Harassment was said to occur in situations when young people were simply 'hanging around' and when they were brought into conflict with police officers even though they had not acted in a way that required police action.

- Action to be taken agreed. Interim meeting arranged to prepare case.

It was agreed that the best way forward was to invite a police representative to discuss the issue and that an interim meeting would be useful to set the agenda for the two-way discussion. The eventual meeting with Inspector Phil Bevan of the South Wales Constabulary was attended by 36 young people, six youth workers, and representatives from NACRO and the Wales Youth Forum. In their interim meeting, the young people had recognised that street confrontations between themselves and the police occurred in an atmosphere of ignorance and mistrust on both sides, and that this problem had to be addressed if the situation was to improve. Inspector Bevan was willing to accept this point and he acknowledged that some officers showed a negative attitude towards the young people. They, in turn, accepted that police officers working on the estate had a difficult job to do and that they might feel threatened when confronted by groups of 15-20 young people, resulting in a 'hard-line' response.

- Agreement reached between young people and outside agency.

There was general agreement that the 'flashpoint' was the actual coming together of police officers and young people on the streets. In these situations both groups tended to be aggressive. The police would be abusive, the young people would react to the abuse and this would lead to official action by the police. The feeling was that if the attitudes of each group towards the other could change, the relationship might improve. Inspector Bevan assured the meeting that he would feed back to local officers and persuade them to be more sympathetic in their approach. At the same time, he required a commitment from the young people that they would:
- try to reduce the incidence of behaviour which resulted in complaints by residents;
- attempt to be less aggressive when approached.

- Arrangements set up for regular meetings.

The young people were willing to comply with these requests and the meeting ended with agreement on both sides that regular meetings should be held between the young people and local police officers to promote deeper levels of understanding and to address other issues of mutual interest.

Evaluation

- Results in clear benefits for young people and local community.

The dialogue between young people and the police set out to address a very specific issue, to involve young people in the process and to lay foundations for a representative forum of young people which could be consulted on a range of issues in the future. The benefits to young people were perceived by youth workers and the young people themselves to be:
- development of communication skills, both verbal (discussion) and written (minutes of meetings and other information);
- the ability to analyse information and make decisions in the light of it;
- an opportunity to express views, particularly with regard to the central issue.

The following quotations from the young people involved were made in response to the question: 'How did the meetings with the police affect you and your friends?'

They moan because we hang around the shopping centre and when we go where no one else is around, by the school and the park, they pull up in cars, flashing their lights and chasing us. They didn't do it so much after the meeting with that bloke.

They chilled out for a while. They still told us to move, but were more friendly.

We were standing at the shopping centre one night and they pulled up, but all they did was beep and wave. It was good, but we did think they were winding us up.

And the police had a response too. This is what Inspector Viv Giles had to say about life after the meetings.

We were receiving complaints about the problem of youth annoyance on the Llanedeyrn estate. On the one hand, residents in the area were complaining bitterly that the police were doing nothing about the problem, while on the other hand the young people in the area were complaining of being perpetually harassed.

The main benefits of the Youth Forum were, in my opinion, education and communication. The young people were informed about the problems they were causing residents and were actively encouraged to behave more responsively and with more consideration for those around them. A lot of them were unaware that their behaviour presented any problem, or even a threat to the local community, and if but one young person now gives pause for thought in the way in which they behave, then the forum has been a success.

The police officers who attended meetings also received an education, in that they encountered a number of articulate young people who were not happy with the way they felt the police were relating to them. And so police officers were similarly called upon to justify themselves.

I feel that it was, and will hopefully continue to be, of benefit to both young people and the police that they can be brought together, communicate with each other and educate each other about their problems.

The problem in relation to young annoyance has not been solved. We still receive calls, although these are in decline at present. Some officers have reported to me that they have received less verbal abuse than was the case and that, upon arriving at the scene of complaints, some young people will now move quietly away once the police have arrived.

The work of the Youth Forum and the local police aimed, in part, to reduce the amount of 'youth annoyance' calls received by the police from local residents. The first meeting with Inspector Bevan took place on 7 May 1991. From June to September 1991, the police received 110 'youth annoyance' calls, compared with 240 for the same period in 1990 – a reduction of 54%.

The case study is particularly useful because it has some feedback from both young people and the police. Clearly, the situation was not entirely resolved by consultation between the two parties, but tension was considerably alleviated. There were quantifiable benefits to the lives of young people in that they felt they had developed new skills during the exercise, and found the police 'more friendly' afterwards. The police felt that the forum was 'of benefit to both young people and the police' and reported a decline in verbal abuse from the young people. Finally, the number of complaints from estate residents fell markedly.

If participation can have this kind of effect in such a polarised situation, imagine the benefits in a less confrontational environment.

The situation suggested in **Exercise 5** (page 21) would give children far more responsibility than was possible with the young people on the Llanedeyrn estate. The exercise should help colleagues think their way through the implications of responsibility, both for the children and for the professionals who must take a back seat.

exercise 3

What does empowerment mean?

Aim
To raise awareness of the meaning of empowerment and its benefits for individuals, and to make a clear connection between definitions of empowerment and reality.

Group size
Part 1: group of colleagues, any size
Part 2: individual
Part 3: individual
Part 4: return to group from Part 1

Materials
Flipchart or OHP (if available), pens and paper

For each part of the exercise, individuals or groups should have access to a sheet with the relevant statements on it, or should be able to see a flipchart or OHP on which the statements are displayed. The statements needed for each part of the exercise are found on the next four pages and can be photocopied. There is no limit to the number of statements that can be chosen in each part of the exercise.

1 The group must agree on the statements which best reflect their idea of empowerment for children. In the course of discussion, the group will not only establish what empowerment is, but also what it is not. This will set the parameters for the rest of the exercise.

2 Using the definition for empowerment that was set out in Part 1, individuals should reflect on the specific circumstances in which they are or have been empowered. They should be encouraged to think of occasions in their childhood as well as adulthood, and may like to add specific instances of real empowerment.

3 Individuals should now focus on one of the environments chosen in Part 2, or on a set of empowering experiences, and reflect on the effect that empowerment had on their subsequent actions and perceptions.

4 The group comes back together and individuals may wish to share some of their findings from parts 2 and 3 before considering the final list of statements. Again, the group must agree on the principles for empowering young people. This will probably be the most difficult part of the exercise.

Evaluation:
The whole exercise should give colleagues a clear sense of whether or not they share concepts of empowerment – or can at least agree on them – and helps to identify where problems may occur if young people are to be empowered.

Note:
Parts 1 and 4 of the exercise can be repeated later on, and may show a change if colleagues' views have altered. The exercise can also be adapted for young people.

15 Professional development

Part 1

Empowerment means:

(a) Getting involved

(b) Having a say

(c) Taking responsibility

(d) Getting power

(e) Being consulted

(f) Taking sole charge

(g) Having your ideas accepted by children and young people

(h) Having your ideas accepted by adults

(i) Changing organisations

(j) Influencing local events

(k) Changing society

(l) Being accepted as an adult

(m) Using your brains

(n) Being trusted

(o) Taking over from adults

(p) Working alongside adults

(q) Training to be an organiser/leader

Any others: _____
_____

Part 2

In which of the following circumstances have you been given a real chance to participate in important decisions?

(a) Your close family

(b) The wider family

(c) School

(d) College

(e) A training programme

(f) Paid employment

(g) Unpaid employment

(h) Trade union or professional association

(i) Youth club or project

(j) Planning an outing for young people

(k) Planning a co-operative venture with young people

(l) Managing and controlling a budget

(m) Serving on a consultative group or committee

(n) Making staff appointments

(o) Contributing to or writing a report

(p) Running or contributing to a campaign

(q) Planning or taking part in a lobby or meeting with political representative

Any other: _____

_____

Part 3

Have your experiences of participation changed you in any of the following ways? (Choose one experience or sequence of events and keep that in mind while considering the statements.)

(a) Increased your knowledge

(b) Increased your skills

(c) Increased your confidence

(d) Helped you to be more effective in giving your point of view

(e) Helped you persuade others to your point of view

(f) Increased your respect for points of view that differ from yours

(g) Lowered your respect for views that differ from yours

(h) Made you see the value of deciding things by committee

(i) Made you doubt the value of deciding things by committee

(j) Given you a better appreciation of the value of money

(k) Made you more skilful in dealing with a range of people

(l) Made you more skilful in dealing with organisations

(m) Strengthened your faith in society as it is

(n) Strengthened your wish to change society

(o) Increased your frustration with situations where you have no influence

(p) Made you respect the ability of people with responsibility

(q) Made you doubt the ability of people with responsibility

Any others: _____

_____

Part 4

Which of these statements should be followed if children and young people are to be empowered?

(a) You cannot have genuine empowerment unless children and young people democratically agree what steps should be taken to introduce empowerment.

(b) Any measure leading to greater empowerment is useful. It is not necessary to go the whole hog right at the start.

(c) Small moves towards empowerment are useless. Children and young people should not agree to be involved unless really significant changes are proposed.

(d) Young people chosen to sit on committees should be elected by children and young people.

(e) It is best for adults to select the children who will sit on committees.

(f) All decision-making bodies for organisations working with children and young people should have children on all their committees.

(g) It is worth starting with one young person's representative on each committee.

(h) On any decision-making committee, at least one third of the members should be children.

(i) On any decision-making committee, at least half the members should be children.

(j) Young people should graduate to more responsibility only by proving themselves.

(k) To introduce genuine empowerment, adults must stand wholly to one side and let children carry through tasks unaided.

(l) If empowerment is to succeed it is essential that children and adults work positively together.

(m) Young people need training before they can be given greater responsibility.

(n) It does not matter what strings are attached, young people should accept all increases in responsibility that are offered to them.

(o) Children should not accept responsibility unless they are fully consulted and accept the terms on which new responsibility is offered.

(p) Young people should not accept responsibility in organisations unless they accept the organisation's policies as a whole.

(q) It is alright to accept responsibility in organisations whose policies you do not agree with, because those policies can be changed.

(r) Children with responsibility should act differently from adults.

(s) Children with responsibility should not be afraid to act the same way as adults.

(t) Change and participation do not necessarily go together.

(u) Young people should use opportunities for empowerment to seek major changes in society.

(v) The best first step towards empowerment is a change in attitude.

(w) The best first step towards empowerment is practical measures, whether or not there is a change in attitude.

Any others: _____

exercise 4

Gains and losses

Aim
To investigate what children and organisations gain and lose when the children are empowered, and to understand the implications of who makes decisions.

Group size
Small groups of no more than 4 people

Materials
Pens and paper

1. Consider the following situation. A hospital has decided to produce an introduction booklet especially for children who are being admitted for the first time. It will explain how the hospital runs, what the children can expect, rules they will have to follow and information about services for children. The board of trustees is willing to spend a considerable amount of money on design and production of the booklet, but they cannot decide whether or not to involve children and young people who are currently patients in writing it.

2. What are the gains and losses of involving current patients with this project? Some suggestions have been entered on the grid below. Discuss these and add any others that occur to you.

	Advantages	Disadvantages
Children and young people	• the booklet would address children's real concerns rather than those which adults think are important • new patients coming in would feel more at home	• children who are particularly unwell may feel left out if they are unable to contribute to something everyone else is doing
Adult professionals	• openly expressed views will help professionals address children's real concerns in the future • these could lead to positive changes in practice later on	• consultation may highlight problems which cannot be solved even in the long term

3. Take an issue of involvement from your own working environment and compile a gains and losses grid for it. Other possible situations might be involving:
   - young people in drawing up the rules for a residential unit;
   - children in designing a local park;
   - children and young people in producing an information pack for their school or residential unit.

4. Once this second grid has been completed, consider the steps which would have to be taken in order to ensure that the children in your environment would have a sufficient understanding of the issues to be effectively involved in making decisions. What steps can be taken now? What steps could be taken in the future? Consider the resource implications.

Evaluation:
The exercise will reveal the perception of gains against losses among professionals. If that perception is weighted very heavily towards losses for professionals and young people, the staff are probably not ready to empower the children they work with and may need more training. A balance that is weighted very heavily towards the gains may indicate that professionals have not yet understood the potential difficulties encountered when involving young people. These should be made evident.

Note:
This activity can be adapted for young people to work on as part of a consultation exercise.

exercise 5

A day out

Aim
To highlight the potential learning outcomes for children and young people who have taken on real responsibility in organising an event.

Group size
Any group of colleagues, but not fewer than 4 people

Materials
Flipchart, pens and paper

1. A small residential unit wants to take all six- to 12-year-olds in their care on a day out during the half-term holiday. The children have been asked where they would most like to go, and the clear winner is a trip to the zoo. Brainstorm what the children might gain from the trip if it is entirely arranged by adults. (Possible answers might be 'a good day out' or 'learning about various animals'.)

2. Now brainstorm what the children might gain if they organise the trip themselves, including obtaining quotes for buses and making a budget. What skills would they need? (Possible answers might be 'communication skills', 'team-building' or 'previous experience of responsibility'.)

3. Brainstorm ideas for how the children might be prepared with the skills which will allow them to plan a trip with confidence. (Possible answers might be 'shared responsibility for tidying rooms throughout the unit', 'answering the unit's telephone' or 'drawing up menus for the unit which would fit into a budget'.)

4. DISASTER! The children arrive at the zoo and it is closed for the day, for refurbishment. Brainstorm the positive and negative outcomes of this experience. (Possible answers might be 'adults have to come up with a snap alternative', 'children have learned never to organise anything without double-checking details'.)

Evaluation:
The trip would have been more easily organised by workers. It would have taken less time, there would have been no need for prior training and workers would have been sure to check whether or not the zoo was actually open on the chosen day. However, the benefits to children of organising the day are measured by the number of learning outcomes, not necessarily by how well or badly the day was run.

21 **Professional** development

3 Tackling the barriers to empowerment

Although empowerment has the potential to benefit children, young people, adults and the wider community, there are several barriers to its success which might prevent an organisation from furthering its programme of involvement, or from implementing one at all. These barriers fall into four broad categories:
- access to decision-making;
- preconceived attitudes (adults' and children's);
- access to information;
- availability of resources.

Before looking at these issues in detail, Checklist 1 provides a rundown of the areas which tend to create problems for empowerment, and any organisation wishing to involve young people should consider these points in relation to their own context. In doing so, it is useful to bear in mind the organisation's structure, the relationships within it (among professionals, among the children, across the two groups, between the organisation and the local authority) and the personalities involved. If the following issues might cause problems, how would they manifest themselves and how could they be solved?

It will be useful to refer back to this checklist as progress is made through the chapter.

Checklist 1 – Potential problem areas

1 Change in culture:
  - meetings with staff and children
  - delegation of responsibilities

2 Cost and time:
  - training
  - resources
  - staff reallocation

3 Fear of failure

4 Professionals' attitudes:
  - users too emotional
  - users unable to make difficult decisions
  - adults better at making decisions

5 Children's attitudes:
  - will they be in line with equal opportunities policy?

6 Organisation's constitution

7 Need for quick decisions

8 Loss of control and power

The **Residential on Elm Street** at the end of this chapter (page 29) is a light-hearted quiz which will help professionals identify some of the dilemmas that can occur when intending to empower young people; dilemmas which in themselves create barriers to participation. Some readers may recognise the events because they are all based on real incidents.

Access to decision-making

The whole culture of an organisation may pose a barrier to participation. For example, meetings and other activities might be conducted in a formal manner which excludes children and young people. The timing for meetings can also be a problem. Workday gatherings immediately exclude children and young people from the decision-making process because children are at school until at least 4.00 pm and young people can be at work placements until 6.00 pm. It may be less convenient for professionals to meet at other times, but if consultation is to be effective it is essential that some, if not all, decisions are made at evening or weekend meetings.

Poor local transport can make it difficult for young people to attend meetings, particularly in rural areas where children may have to travel quite a distance and where the last bus home often leaves before the meeting starts. The venue chosen for meetings can also be a problem. All too often, meetings with children take place at a venue where professionals feel comfortable, even though children are more likely to feel at ease on their own territory. As it is children who most need confidence in this new situation, it is up to the professionals to make this concession. For instance, a local authority is more likely to have a productive consultation with young people if their meeting is held in a local café or community centre rather than in the council chamber with its formal seating and imposing emblem on the wall.

Similarly, individual children participating in a review meeting may feel more confident in their own residential unit, or some other familiar context, than in a social services' meeting room. They must feel able to question the presence of any adults who attend the meeting and to request that inappropriate adults leave. For instance, children in foster care may find the presence of their foster parents at review meetings makes it difficult for them to make an honest contribution, in which case they might wish to have the parents excluded for at least part of the meeting.

The means by which a meeting or conference is conducted must also accommodate children and young people. More frequent breaks give groups an opportunity to evaluate a meeting, while individuals can use the time to consult with their advocate. Unless a really glowing speaker can be found, it is also a good idea to drop the welcome speech by a local dignitary as it can give the impression that the forthcoming conference will be nothing more than a boring endurance test.

When working with groups, access to decision-making is significantly improved if the young people have a chance to gel before being taken into the process. Residential training events are perfect for creating a close group, but where these are not possible, good assertiveness training and work on group decision-making is essential (Part 2 of this manual has some ideas for training exercises). The ratio of children to adults must be carefully balanced because, if there are too many adults, the children will not feel in a strong enough position to speak freely.

Preconceived attitudes

It may be argued that the main barriers to empowerment are the attitudes of professionals and other adults. Some of the common myths about children and young people are that they:
- don't really want to be involved;
- are not representative;
- are irrational;
- are unreasonable;
- are too emotional.

In reality, many children and young people do want to be involved in making decisions which affect them. Most of them are neither irrational nor too emotional and, when given detailed information such as budget limitations, they are not generally unreasonable. Nobody can be entirely representative but, as with the rest of the population, it is possible for children to represent a group with an interest in a particular issue.

The attitudes of individual professionals are as crucial to the success or failure of empowerment as the general perceptions held across an organisation, if not more so. During consultations with the Children's Rights Development Unit it became clear that for many children, their views of care were determined by their relationship with the social worker, while young people who occasionally truanted from school said that the decision whether or not to attend a class depended almost entirely on who would be teaching it rather than on the subject being taught. It is not possible to say precisely why children and young people are able to relate to some professionals and not others. Certainly, there must be some aspect of personality – everyone gets on with some people better than others – but it is likely that professionals' attitudes towards individual children and young people in general also have a considerable part to play in the success of a relationship.

Exercises 6 and 7 (pages 31 and 33) both investigate attitudes towards children, one through literature and the other through active role play. Both of them can be adapted for use with young people.

As participation requires young people and professionals to cooperate, it is essential that the professionals involved have a generally positive attitude towards young people, and that the young people are able to detect it. It is also important that the young people have a positive attitude towards the adult professionals with whom they will work. If not, they could derail their own participation before it even starts. Examples of negative views might be that adults:
- never listen;
- will not give us responsibility;
- think we don't know anything;
- are out of touch;
- do not understand us.

It is the responsibility of professionals to ensure that views like these have no basis in fact. An awareness of the elements which might discourage children and young people from participation (see Checklist 2) will help with this.

> **Checklist 2**
>
> **Things which put children and young people off participation**
>
> 1. Fear of being stigmatised
> 2. Social security problems (not being available for work due to meetings)
> 3. Lack of confidence or skills
> 4. Rigid constitutions
> 5. Committee structure
> 6. Rigid culture of organisation
> 7. Exclusive language and terminology
> 8. Lack of information
> 9. Lack of training
> 10. Lack of access to phones, computers and other resources
> 11. Unsuitable refreshments
> 12. Political correctness
> 13. Only one or two children allowed to participate
> 14. Lack of support or back-up from a group of young people
> 15. Insufficient resources and staff to provide support
> 16. Adults refuse to give up any power
> 17. Young people not allowed to handle money (most usually, in local authority projects)
> 18. Lack of transport
> 19. Lack of feedback after one-off consultation

Access to information

Adults get their information in many ways: through conferences, courses and residential training sessions, professional organisations, magazines, formal meetings and even conversations in the pub. They are constantly bombarded by information and can discriminate between the details they wish to keep and the details they wish to discard.

By comparison, children and young people rarely have direct access to information networks. This puts them at a clear disadvantage (they are effectively *dis*empowered before they even start) and it is up to the professionals who do receive information to ensure that the children see it too. Young people will be empowered to act only if they can actually see copies of complaints procedures, or read details of the local 'In Care' group, or get information about events or conferences that they could attend. With a little training, they can then go one step further and start to obtain the information for themselves.

The use of jargon may be another barrier to receiving information and can prevent children from feeling part of an organisation's decision-making structure. Many youth workers use social policy speak as a kind of shorthand, but as one of the consequences of jargon is to identify who 'belongs' and who does not, it is hardly surprising when young people feel excluded by it. If children are to be given written and verbal information on which to base their views, professionals must ensure that the information is expressed in a way which seeks positively to include young people. If children are then to attend meetings and be able to express those views, it is important that everyone at the meeting can participate fully in the discussion.

Pre-meetings and evaluations

The absence of jargon alone is not enough to ensure the inclusion of children and young people in making decisions. It is no good simply to pretend that children are uninitiated adults; they need time and space to discuss the issues in a pre-meeting, with a support person if they feel it appropriate. The pre-meeting:

- provides a safe environment in which children have the time to clarify issues and explore some possible solutions to present in the later meeting;
- is an opportunity to read papers, interpret acronyms and identify the role of other organisations so that the later meeting will not have to be interrupted by questions of clarification;
- helps to prevent some of the group feeling disempowered by having to ask for clarification;
- is a chance to find out about the other people who will be at the meeting, who they are, what they do, their 'politics', and whether there are any strong dislikes between individuals.

Group evaluations after a meeting help establish whether children need any more information to fill in gaps from the main meeting and whether they would prefer meetings to be structured differently. Where the membership of the group of children and young people attending is constant, the need for pre-meetings and evaluations tends to decline.

Briefings

It is vital that individual young people are properly briefed if they are to be involved in a decision which could change the course of their lives, say at a review meeting. Such a briefing should include discussion about why the meeting is being held, who will attend it, the options that are likely to be explored, the young person's role and rights (independent advocacy and appeal, for instance), how they would like their view put across – and by whom.

There is a danger that a briefing can become just another daunting meeting, and so it may work best in a familiar informal setting, such as a local McDonald's, or over a game of cards.

Availability of resources

This chapter has discussed the need for changes in culture, rescheduling of meetings, special training and the generation of specific information. All of these cost money – either as direct expenses or in terms of workers' time – and any organisation wanting to involve young people must ensure that it has the necessary financial resources to allow participation before making a start. This includes being able to pay for several children to attend meetings, not just one or two, and must include travel and other expenses in the reckoning. Expenses must always be available in cash on the day, or in advance.

Funding must be applied for at an early stage and it is advisable to involve children in the application, thereby giving the long-term programme of empowerment an exciting kick start.

Equal opportunities

Some groups of children and young people face further barriers to empowerment and may need greater resources and commitment, for instance those who are disaffected, who suffer racism or who are gay or lesbian. **Exercise 8** (page 34) provides an opportunity to consider issues of access from the point of view of young black people, and the questions can be adapted if professionals wish to think about the services they are providing for other user groups. Extra issues for children with disabilities include meeting in places with wheelchair access, the welcome they receive, the impression given by images in the building (posters and other materials) and whether the people they meet understand their needs and know how to offer assistance. For example:

- do posters, books and children's playthings show positive images of disabled people?
- are staff able to use sign language – British Sign Language (BSL) or Makaton?
- do staff understand the use of other communication devices, such as pictorial symbol boards or electronic voice systems?
- does everyone understand the needs of people who use hearing aids (reduce background noise, don't shout, improve acoustics) or who lipread (speak slowly and clearly, don't cover mouth or turn away, have the light shining on your face)?
- how is information for project users produced – is it available in large print, audiotape, braille and text supported by Rebus or Makaton symbols?

It is impossible for this manual to cover all the issues for empowering all children and young people. However, there are several excellent books to refer to, including: *Anti-Bias Curriculum: Tools for Empowering Young Children* (Derman-Sparks 1989), *Disability Equality in the Classroom: A Human Rights Issue* (Rieser and Mason 1992), *Inclusion, the Way Forward: A guide to integration for young disabled children* (Mason 1993), *Invisible Children: Report of the Joint Conference on Children, Images and Disability* (Rieser 1995), *Playing Fair: a parents' guide to tackling discrimination.* Details of these and other books can be found on page 95.

Identify the barriers in your organisation

The barriers to empowerment will manifest themselves differently in every organisation, depending on the existing power structure and the individuals involved. It is helpful to consider the reasons why children have not been involved before and **Exercise 9** (page 35) provides an opportunity to look at these problems in detail and to consider methods of rectifying them. Copies of checklists 1 and 2 can act as *aides memoire* when working through the exercise. Checklist 3 is a summary of the points in this chapter and it will be a particularly helpful reference for Exercise 9.

Checklist 3 – Avoiding the common barriers to participation

1 Ensure there is real access to decision-making:
   - hold meetings in places where children and young people feel comfortable, not in formal adult surroundings
   - meetings should take place at times and dates when children can attend
   - young people should be able to get to and from the meeting on public transport
   - do not use jargon
   - do not patronise children and young people
   - provide refreshments
   - provide expenses in cash
   - take care to balance the number of children to the number of adults
   - provide assertiveness training for children and young people
   - arrange a residential to help the group bond and allow for training
   - consider the specific access needs for young black people; young women; young gay men and lesbians; children with special needs; working class children; disaffected young people

2 Be aware of adults' potentially negative attitudes such as:
   - 'We have always done it this way'
   - 'We have always met on a Monday morning'
   - 'It's easier if I do it myself'
   - 'It's not their place to make decisions'
   - 'We're dealing with serious politics here'
   - 'The children have to earn our respect'
   - 'They are irrational'
   - 'They don't really want to be involved'
   - 'They lack knowledge and experience'
   - 'We tried it once before'
   - 'The young people are too emotive'

3 Change working practices so that there is no foundation to young people's potentially negative attitudes, such as:
   - 'You don't really want to know what I think'
   - 'I can't be bothered because nothing useful will happen'
   - 'They tried it before but no one was really listening'
   - 'You won't give me any real power'
   - 'All the workers are out of touch'
   - 'You don't understand us'

4 Provide real access to information:
   - cut out all jargon in speech and written materials
   - always remind children of forthcoming meetings, as many of them do not carry diaries
   - brief young people fully on adult committee members prior to the first meeting
   - arrange pre-meetings to allow for briefing and discussion
   - arrange post-meetings for evaluation
   - stop official meetings to clarify any acronyms and names
   - address all correspondence to the children, not to their parents or carers

5 Ensure availability of financial resources for the following:
   - funds to involve several people, not a token one or two
   - expenses in cash on the day
   - hire of meeting places
   - funds to take action which has been agreed on, or to contact the people who can provide such funds
   - staff time

Residential on Elm Street

This is a light-hearted quiz for those working with young people. All the questions are based on real incidents. There are no scores in this quiz.

1. Your are planning a residential event. Do you:
   - write the rules and post them in advance to all delegates?
   - set up a consultation with young people about the rules?
   - establish ground rules on the first night of the residential, by having a whole group meeting?
   - establish ground rules by dealing with crises on the first night?

2. One young person arrives with an over-protective parent. Do you:
   - send the pair of them home?
   - accept the parent's right to be with their child?
   - think up menial tasks for the parent to be given, allowing the young person space to participate?
   - negotiate with them separately and together to reach a compromise?

3. You believe that a party is being held by young people in a third-floor room. Do you:
   - knock on the door and remind them of the rules?
   - scale the outside of the building and jump through the window?
   - go to your room and pretend to be asleep?
   - start a party of your own?

4. A young person vomits out of a third-floor window on to a co-worker's car. Do you:
   - laugh a lot and deny any knowledge of the event?
   - laugh a lot and get the young person to clear up the mess?
   - send the young person home?
   - tell your co-worker immediately?

5. One of the workshops has just started and the facilitators are missing (they are hiding at the back of the workshop!). Do you:
   - cancel the workshop?
   - organise small group discussions and search for the missing facilitators?
   - run an impromptu puppet show featuring your hands as Sooty and Sweep while other people search for the facilitators?
   - cry?

6. One of the young people at your event is assaulted by an adult from a group sharing the facilities. Do you:
   - counsel the young person and inform them of their rights?
   - demand to see the centre mamâger?
   - call the police?
   - confront the other group's coordinator?

7 You become aware that the young people have stolen goods from a local shop. Do you:
   - call the police?
   - call your line manager?
   - call a meeting for the whole group to discuss options?
   - call for a fair distribution of the proceeds?

8 A young person boldly announces to you that they have just had sexual intercourse. Do you:
   - offer them a cigarette?
   - offer them advice about safe sex and privacy?
   - smile, as your icebreakers have obviously worked (see pages 44–7)?
   - try to ignore the issue completely?

9 A young person speaks to you in confidence and discloses that they are gay. Do you:
   - offer them a cigarette?
   - offer them advice about safe sex and privacy?
   - offer them personal support and signpost them to appropriate agencies?
   - support the young person by announcing it to the whole group?

10 At the end of the residential, social workers fail to pick up two of the young people. They live approximately 100 miles away. Do you:
   - phone the duty social service number?
   - wait with them until someone arrives?
   - give them some change and a road map?
   - cry?

exercise 6

Adults with attitude

Aim
To examine views of the relationship between children and adults, and discuss how these views might affect empowerment.

Group size
Part 1: group of any size
Part 2: individuals
Parts 3-6: same group as Part 1

Materials
Flipchart, paper and pens

1 Write the following quotation on a piece of flipchart paper, but without the name of the author and the date (it was written by Socrates, *circa* 300 BC). Ask the group who they think might have said this, and when. This activity should set the tone for the whole exercise.

> 'The young people of today love luxury. They have bad manners, they scoff at authority and lack respect for their elders. Children nowadays are real tyrants, they no longer stand up when their elders come into the room where they are sitting, they contradict their parents, chat together in the presence of adults, eat gluttonously and tyrannise their teachers.'

2 Look at the following quotations and decide, on a scale of 0 to 10, how much you agree with the statement (when 0 is 'strongly disagree' and 10 is 'strongly agree'). Your score should be based on your immediate response to the quotation and should be as honest as possible.

(a) 'I've seen kids ride bicycles, run, play ball, set up a camp, swing, fight a war, swim and race for eight hours ... yet have to be driven to the garbage can.'
   Erma Bombeck, *If Life is a Bowl of Cherries – What am I Doing in the Pits?*, 1978

(b) 'Oh what a tangled web do parents weave
When they think that their children are naive.'
   Ogden Nash, 'Baby, What Makes the Sky Blue?', 1940

(c) 'I never met a kid I liked.'   **W. C. Fields**

(d) 'This would be a better world for children if parents had to eat spinach.'
   Groucho Marx, *Animal Crackers*

(e) 'The business of a child interests a child not at all. Children very rarely play at being other children.'
   David Holloway, *The Daily Telegraph*, 1966

(f) 'Children have never been very good at listening to their elders, but they have never failed to imitate them. They must, they have no other models.'
   James Baldwin, *Nobody Knows My Name*

(g) 'There is no end to the violations committed by children on children when talking alone.'
   Elizabeth Bowen, *House in Paris*, 1935

(h) 'Parents love their children more than children love their parents.'
   Auctoritates Aristotelis, medieval writer

31 Professional development

(i) 'Grown-ups never understand anything for themselves, and it is tiresome for children to be always and forever explaining things to them.'
Antoine de Saint-Exupéry, *The Little Prince*, 1943

(j) 'No matter how old a mother is she watches her middle-aged children for signs of improvement.'
Florida Scott-Maxwell, *Measure of my Days*, 1968

3   Come together as a group of colleagues, compare responses, discuss reasons for them and agree on a group scoring for each quotation.

4   Take each quotation and discuss the implications for empowering young people if the statement were considered to be absolutely true (for instance, if all adults disliked all children, along with W. C. Fields, would they be likely to involve them in decisions?).

5   Take the group's score for each quotation and discuss these in relation to what was said in Part 3. (For instance, if the group scored 0 on the W. C. Fields quotation, it would suggest that everyone has met a lot of children they like, suggesting that they might be able to work well with them. A score of 5 might indicate that professionals have met several children they like and several they dislike, which might indicate that their willingness to involve children will depend entirely upon the individual child.)

6   Once the exercise has been completed, read the following poem, written by a young person.

> I opened my mouth, I spoke
> Everyone stopped and stared
> 'Hold On, Hold On!'
> was the chairperson's greeting,
> 'I presume Adults are running this meeting.
> You're just a child, we know what's best
> I am sure we'll come to some agreement.'
> I felt like screaming, but what could be done?
> After all this system can't be beaten.
> I wasn't there, just an illusion.
> Talking to the walls, still nobody noticed.
> Before I knew it, my life had been planned
> What's the point of me in this meeting?
> I began to rebel, I wanted to be heard
> But to them I was a problem,
> a reject example of a human being.
> I wanted someone to come through the door
> with listening ears.
> Someone who understood my fears.
> The things that should have been said
> by this reject human being,
> are really quite full of meaning.
>
> Chrissie Elms-Bennett

Ask the group for their immediate responses to these words. Does the poem ring true? Does it put any of the earlier quotations into context, and does it have an effect on any of the scores that the group came up with? You may also find the poem useful in working with children and young people, again to ascertain immediate responses.

Evaluation:
The exercise may bring out some views that surprise the group. Participants will then have an opportunity to explore these views. The ability of the group to agree on scores will also show how well they work as a team – an essential skill if they are to empower young people effectively.

exercise 7

Role plays

Aim
To explore the way in which professionals perceive their relationship with children and young people.

Group size
Part 1: pairs
Part 2: pairs, leading into groups of 4 or 6
Part 3: groups of 3 to 6

In role play, groups get together and improvise a given situation using what they know of the personalities that might be involved and the ways they react. The outcome of a role play depends very much on the perceptions of those involved and can reveal a great deal about their preconceived attitudes. Participants may be a little uncomfortable with the idea to begin with, but several groups of colleagues can role play at the same time and there is no need for anyone else necessarily to 'see' what they are doing.

1. A Year 7 class teacher and pupil are meeting to discuss arrangements for a forthcoming trip to the theatre (Year 7 is the first year in secondary school, that is 11/12 year olds). The pupil is the elected representative for the class. So far, the play has been chosen and the tickets booked. Money for the trip is currently being collected, the coach needs to be booked and arrangements made for where everyone will meet. Role play the conversation between teacher and pupil as they discuss what has happened so far, and make plans for the other arrangements.

   At the end, swap roles and role play the same situation, but set it in a youth club. The meeting is now between a young person and a youth worker.

2. A meeting between a child and a social worker half an hour prior to a review meeting. The child is in residential care and wants to stay there, but the social worker and his/her colleagues think the child would be better off in foster care. They have already discussed the issue, but this is the first time the child has been included in the discussions. What tactics for persuasion does each individual use? Remember that there is a significant time limit on the meeting, and that a final decision on the child's immediate future will be made in half an hour's time.

   When this role play is completed, pairs should form themselves into groups of four or six. Each pair should perform their role play to the larger group, which will then discuss the performances and decide on the most realistic situation. The group will then role play the review meeting which, all along, has been scheduled for 30 minutes after the pre-meeting. One member of the group plays the child.

3. A group of young people is drawing up a list of five big forthcoming events for their youth club. The club meets twice a week and these events are to occur over the next three months. The group is deciding how many of the events will be on-site, how many will be trips, where the money will come from to fund the events and – most important of all – what the events are to be. They cannot agree on anything. Some of the group want all the events to be educational, others just want to have fun. There is a disagreement and a youth worker intervenes. Role play the situation from the start of the meeting. What happens when the worker steps in?

Evaluation:
If groups want to show each other the situation they have worked out, then they can. Otherwise, it is possible simply to discuss the outcomes that occurred.

In Part 1, it will be most interesting to find out who was controlling the trip. Who had booked the theatre? Who was collecting the money? Who was reporting back to whom? Was the pupil contacting coach companies, or was the teacher doing it all? Is there any room in the teacher/pupil relationship for children to be given real control over events such as this? What differences were there between the teacher/pupil role play and the young person/ youth worker role play? What assumptions might lie behind those differences?

In Part 2, how much did the social worker role use prior knowledge, experience and discussion with colleagues to sway the child's position? Did the social worker provide the child with real information on which he/she could make an informed decision? Was the child's point of view really taken into consideration at either the pre-meeting or the review meeting? Was the child able to change the social workers' minds. Knowledge is power in this exercise. Who uses it, and how?

In Part 3, did the youth worker take over, or were the young people able/allowed to resolve their dispute? Did the youth worker attempt to control the young people? Did they need controlling? The way that role playing professionals characterise the young people will, in itself, be telling. For instance, how serious was the 'disagreement'? An argument which got entirely out of hand and had to be resolved by the youth worker suggests that professionals regard young people as unreasonable. A heated discussion that the young people were able to resolve through the youth worker's mediation suggests something more cooperative.

exercise 8

Tackling racism

Aim
To discuss issues of access and involvement of young black people in an organisation and think about ways of improving the situation.

Group size
Part 1: individuals or groups of 3 to 4
Part 2: unlimited size

Materials
One copy of the grid per person/small group. A blackboard/flipchart with the nine questions below written out

1. Ask the individuals/small groups to consider the following questions with reference to your organisation. They are to think about whether or not there is clear access to the organisation for young black people, and must enter the current situation regarding each question on to the grid. If that situation is less than satisfactory, the groups should enter on the grid their suggestions for improvements in the short, medium and long term.

   - What support does your organisation offer to young black people?
   - Are the opening times for your organisation convenient for young black people to attend?
   - Are your committee meetings at convenient times for young black people to attend?
   - Do your activities and events reflect the lives and concerns of young black people?
   - Does your organisation run any activities specifically for young black people?
   - How is publicity for your organisation made available to young black people?
   - How inviting are your surroundings for young black people?
   - What is your organisation's reputation in the black community?
   - Does your organisation have anything in its constitution or other documentation which attempts to safeguard the rights of young people from racism?

   For instance, if the organisation is a drop-in advice centre with opening times that clash with those of a local club for young black people, the drop-in centre might modify its opening times in the short term, consult with the club in the medium term and in the long term may work out a co-operative relationship with the youth club which helps direct the young people to the advice centre's services.

2. Once individuals or small groups have completed their grids, bring everyone together to discuss their ideas for short-, medium- and long-term action. The whole group should agree on their strategies, and this session could then provide the basis for real action to be taken.

exercise 9

Identifying the barriers

Aim
To identify the different barriers that children and young people would face when moving towards participation in your organisation.

Group size
Any number of colleagues, but no fewer than 3 people

Materials
Flipchart, paper and pens. Copies of checklists 1, 2 and 3 (pages 22, 25 and 28)

1   Bearing in mind the level of participation that interests your organisation, brainstorm the barriers that would face the children and young people with whom you work in achieving that participation. List specific problems under the general headings of:

    - access to decision-making;
    - preconceived attitudes (adults' and children's);
    - access to information;
    - availability of resources.

2   Discuss what changes need to take place in order to overcome these problems.

3   Discuss what methods and resources must be employed to implement these changes, and consider whether the organisation has the money to achieve them. If not, can the necessary funds be generated?

part 2
working with children and young people

4 Preparing children and young people for involvement

Children must be able to see what they're getting out of participation to sustain an interest in it, whatever their reasons for wanting to take part. The reasons will obviously differ from one child to another, but will probably stem initially from an interest in achieving change. Whether it is membership of a school council, contributing to a forum for young people looked after by the local authority, the creation of a local environment group or participating in a consultative exercise by an organisation seeking to develop its services for young people, the originating interest is likely to be a desire to make a difference to the status quo. It is therefore extremely important that in helping to create opportunities for participation, every effort is made to be realistic about the scope of young people's participation, the potential for change and the likely timescales involved.

For many young people, the motivation for continuing involvement will be strengthened by the personal benefits of being involved in an organisation or community activity:
- acquiring new skills;
- experience that could be put to use in future employment;
- greater responsibility;
- new challenges;
- a worthwhile activity;
- an extended social life.

Other young people might see involvement as a route towards future voluntary work, whilst others who have, for example, experienced abuse or life in care, might wish to use that experience to help others.

There is also a third group – survivor groups – for whom participation and empowerment can have a therapeutic effect. Many survivor groups, particularly those for sexually abused girls and young women, have shown the benefits of running autonomous and confidential forums.

Bonding the group and building a team

There is no secret formula for working with a group of children or young people, though success or failure often rests on professionals' ability to assess their own performance. Group dynamics also have an effect, and workers must take these into account at the same time as they consider the children's individual needs, cultures and attention spans. It always helps to recognise that tangible results will take some time, particularly when working with groups of disaffected young people.

> **Checklist 4**
> **Points to remember when working with children and young people**
>
> 1 Be honest
>
> 2 Listen to criticism
>
> 3 Be open and approachable
>
> 4 Keep a sense of humour
>
> 5 Treat children with respect
>
> 6 Do not patronise
>
> 7 Do not prejudge
>
> 8 Be non-judgmental
>
> 9 Learn from your mistakes
>
> 10 Take account of young people's needs
>
> 11 Be flexible
>
> 12 Do not expect the children to lavish you with thanks

By far the best way to help a group bond and build trust between individuals is to provide opportunities for them to socialise with each other. This is easily done if all the group members live locally and if there is time in hand before directly involving young people in decision-making. In these circumstances, a visit to the skating rink or bowling alley gives everyone the opportunity to help each other with skating or bowling techniques, and everyone will have had to agree on the time and place to meet.

However, socialising may not be possible if individuals do not live near one another, or if they have never met before and have come together for a limited period only – for instance, at a conference. In these circumstances, the group must gel as quickly as possible and the best way to do this is through **Icebreaker Exercises**, a selection of which are given at the end of this chapter (pages 44–7).

The following case study shows how icebreakers can be chosen to highlight issues that will come up later. It goes on to show how these exercises can lead into others which help children learn cooperation and group discussion techniques, all of which prepare them for future involvement in decision-making.

case study

Workshop with children about the UN Convention on the Rights of the Child

Several organisations in Scotland decided to hold a one-day event with children to explore their rights. The organisations involved were The Scottish Child Law Centre, Strathclyde Regional Council Social Work Department, Easterhouse Child Centred Project, the Children's Rights Service, Who Cares? Scotland, and Woodcraft Folk Strathclyde Project.

- Aim to raise awareness of children's rights and prepare for further involvement of children.

The day was intended to establish the concept of children's rights from the perspective of children themselves, and was the first part of a range of activities aimed at producing resource materials for use by children's groups and schools. There could be no expectation to involve the children in decision-making during just one day. Instead, the intention was to raise children's awareness of rights and to help them into a position where they would be prepared for involvement later on. They would also be able to go back to their schools and pass on what they had learned to others. Twenty-five children aged between seven and nine attended the workshop.

The day's programme

- Use of icebreakers to relax participants and raise issues.

After informal registration, the children were asked to make name badges. Apart from the obvious need for participants to be easily identifiable and for them to get to know each other, this exercise was a creative way into the concept of having the right to a name. It was followed by an introduction to the day and some icebreaker games which successfully helped to relax the participants. This part of the programme was concluded with some parachute games and rounds of Chinese Whispers designed to highlight the importance of listening.

- Imaginative exercises used to raise issues.

Moving on to more serious work, the children took part in an exercise around the idea of emotions which the organisers felt was the simplest way to evoke the concept of rights. The room was divided into four sections, using lines on the floor, and each section was given an emotion as its title. There were two positive emotions: 'Happy', 'Excited'; and two negative emotions: 'Sad', 'Worried'. All participants moved around the room to music and when it stopped the section they were in became their 'chosen' emotion. They were then given a scenario – 'At the Doctor's', 'In the School Playground', 'In a Strange Place' or 'Going to McDonald's' – and asked to imagine a reason why they might experience their 'chosen' emotion in that scenario. It was hoped that the children's responses would relate to some of the fundamental rights laid out in the UN Convention: the right to a home; the right to medical attention; the right to food; and the right to be safe.

- Issues raised linked to UN convention.

In practice, this session exceeded the organisers' expectations. Many issues were raised that highlighted a particular right. These were written into 'clouds' and displayed around the room. Among the issues raised were:
- bullying;
- safety;
- the right to food;
- the right to medical attention;
- the right to play;
- the right to protection;
- the right to go to school.

The first session in the afternoon began with the Farmyard Game, a crazy game designed to divide the children into groups of five so that small group work could commence. Each participant was given a card with an animal printed on it, there being five different animal cards distributed equally between the children. With their eyes closed, everyone in the group then started moving around the room making their creature's noise until they had found the other four children who were making the same noise. These were the groups they worked in for the rest of the day.

- Children look at issues through exercises based on cooperation and sharing.

The groups were then asked to do an exercise which relied on cooperation, sharing and taking notice of others in the group. Each participant was given a number of cards cut into various shapes, and each group of five had enough

40 Empowering children and young people

- Creative methods used to raise awareness of children's rights.

- Use of child-friendly evaluation exercises.

cards to make five squares of equal size, but no single child could make a square from their own shapes. Individuals had to work together to put the right pieces together, but they were not allowed to speak nor to take shapes from one another. Pieces had to be offered. The exercise achieved an excellent rapport between the children, particularly noticeable at this point because the groups had been purposefully composed of participants from different schools.

This led to the afternoon's main workshop in which groups used UNICEF posters and various photographs to discuss the idea of rights. There were additional prompts used by those leading the discussions, including cards with each of the main Convention rights as well as questions such as: When do you say 'it's not fair' or 'why can't I ...'? Children were then asked to design posters or write a short story about rights.

At the end of the day, the children took part in an evaluation exercise, the first part of which was a game. Various signs were put up around the room, with comments ranging from 'Garbage' to 'Mega Brilliant'. Each part of the programme was called out, including play and lunch, and the children ran to whichever comment best described what they thought about that item. In the second part of the evaluation children were asked to write or draw their own comments on to large sheets of paper which were then displayed around the room. Their comments included:

- 'Today was brilliant. I liked it. I will be glad to do it again.'
- 'Was brill, better than doing sums.'
- 'I liked the games and the food.'
- 'The Mighty Monsters was excellent. It was good fun. I liked lunch and when we looked at the pictures and talked about everything.'
- 'I liked burgers, games, art work. Didn't like: end of day.'

Building a team and negotiating the ground rules

As the case study shows, once the icebreaker exercises had allowed the group to feel more comfortable with each other, it was important to build the team through cooperation – and this was done using the squares game. Note that all the exercises during the day were aimed at highlighting specific issues or at creating a bond between group members, and also note how each game built upon the one before it. **Exercise 10** (page 48) is aimed at bonding the group at the end of a session, and leaving them with a positive memory to hold on to until next time.

If consultation is to work over the long term, young people also need a set of ground rules. It must be clear what they are being offered and that the rules are there to help everyone work together towards that aim. This issue is particularly important when a group is volatile and when there is a risk that some of the individuals may not get on well together.

Article 12, the children's rights group which is run by children and young people (see Foreword), established the ground rules for conduct as soon as they were formed. Those ground rules are given below. There is one set which all young people must agree to follow and another set which all adults invited to meetings or involved with Article 12 must agree to follow. In this way, the ground rules represent a mutual contract. It is worth noting that the adult ground rules are more prohibitive than those guiding the young people, to ensure that adults are not able to take more control than would be appropriate in this organisation.

Young people's ground rules
1 We all respect each other's point of view.
2 We listen when someone else is talking in a meeting.
3 There should be no illegal substances present at any of the meetings.
4 All present at the meeting will not drink alcohol.

5. All present at the meeting will not smoke unless the whole group has consented.
6 If someone wants to sleep then the other members should not prevent them from doing this.
7 Young people can ask adults to leave meetings.
8 People will respect the chairperson.

Adult ground rules
1 Adults may not speak in meetings or read Article 12 papers outside meetings without the permission of members.
2 Adult council members may not decide Article 12 policy or priorities except in circumstances where the adult member is at risk of becoming financially or criminally liable.
3 The adult's role is to inform, advise and assist members of Article 12.
4 Adults may give their views but may not demand or pressure that their view is accepted.
5 Adults may not withhold information relevant to Article 12.
6 Adults must not act on behalf of Article 12 without instruction from members.
7 Adults may not drink alcohol at meetings.
8 Adults may not smoke without the consent of the whole group at meetings.

Another example of ground rules which empower young people are those used by Caldercliffe residential home for older teenagers, shown in Figure 4.1. The unit provides young people with clear reasons for imposing its non-negotiable rules, and this shows a respect for their need to know and understand issues that directly affect their lives. Furthermore, these non-negotiable rules are balanced by a complementary set of negotiable rules. The reasons behind these rules are also provided, as are the parameters for negotiation. In this way, the young people know where their power lies and understand how to use it.

Exercises 11 to **13** (pages 49 to 51) help to establish ground rules. **Exercise 13** has some contractual aspects to it, though it is concentrated on individual rights rather than individual responsibilities. This exercise could be adapted to help workers and young people agree on a contract. **Exercise 14** (page 52) then moves groups of children or young people towards real cooperative thinking.

All the exercises in this chapter are forms of initial training which prepare children for informed involvement in decision-making.

Figure 4.1

NON-NEGOTIABLE RULES

Rule	Reason
Discriminating behaviour and language, bullying, violence, etc, is not acceptable and will be challenged.	This is for the protection of yourself and others. It will help to promote harmony. It is also about showing respect for others and their beliefs. Besides being socially unacceptable, it is also Kirklees policy.
Weapons and tools are not allowed in the unit.	Besides being dangerous they are illegal. It will also protect property from damage. Socially unacceptable. Also for the protection of other people.
Stolen property is not allowed on the premises.	Legal reasons.
Drugs, alcohol, solvent abuse are prohibited.	These are not allowed on the premises. Firstly because drugs and solvent abuse are illegal and dangerous to health. Also, Kirklees policy and Health & Safety reasons.
Stealing is not allowed.	Stealing is illegal and socially unacceptable.
There must be no intentional criminal damage to items in the unit and its structure.	Criminal damage is illegal and socially unacceptable.
18+ videos/computer games are not allowed in the unit	This is illegal, and Kirklees policy.
You will be expected to participate in regular fire drills.	This is for your health and safety, so you know what to do if there is a fire, or we have to evacuate the building for whatever reason.
Friends visiting: 6.00-9.00pm Mon-Fri. Any two hours between 2.00 and 9.00pm Sat-Sun. Maximum: five visitors at any one time. Visitors not allowed upstairs.	Health and safety, fire regulations. Your visitors will not be allowed upstairs. This is because, in the past, property has gone missing.

NEGOTIABLE RULES

Rule	Negotiation	Reason
Cooking Mon-Thurs. No gas cooker past 10.00pm. Kitchen closed 11.00pm.	Fri-Sun, closing the kitchen may be extended at the discretion of the staff.	Health and safety; fire regulations.
Bedtimes 11.15pm Sun-Thurs.	Fri and Sat, later at staff's discretion.	Education, work, career etc.
TV 4.30-11.00pm Mon-Thurs.	Fri-Sun, earlier/later at staff's discretion.	Education, work, career etc.
Games room (incl. Sega) 4.30-10.00pm Mon-Fri.	Sat and Sun to be negotiated.	Education, work, career etc.
Visits 6.00-9.00pm Mon-Fri Any two hours between 2.00 and 9.00pm Sat-Sun Maximum: five visitors at any one time. Visitors not allowed upstairs.	Family and foster parent visit totally negotiable. Staff to reserve right to ask visitors to leave.	Others require privacy; health and safety; fire regulations; behaviour of guests; theft from other residents.
Laundry End at 9.00pm. In case of emergency, ask staff.	Frequency to be negotiated.	Health and safety; fire regulations; security problem.
Privacy Do not go into rooms uninvited or unannounced.	Staff reserve the right to enter if it's felt that safety and security are at risk.	Safety; security; health and hygiene; legal reasons.
Getting up time Mon-Fri 9.00am.	Sat, Sun, holidays, shift work negotiable.	Education, work, career etc.
Smoking 15 year olds cannot smoke on the premises. No smoking in bedrooms.	Smoking areas to be negotiated.	Smoking policy; health and safety; fire regulations.
Staying out Sun-Thurs to be in at 11.00pm.	Fri and Sat, negotiable if not considered missing/absconded	Security; safety; legal reasons.

exercises

Quick icebreaker exercises

Aims

All of the following icebreakers are intended to help the individuals in a group of children get to know each other and the professionals involved. They also encourage the group to gel and begin working together.

Group size

All the icebreakers are designed to work with any number of people, though each will work better in some contexts than others. Workers should choose the exercises that are most appropriate to their group dynamic and the individuals within the group.

Name games

1 **Name and adjective**

   This game helps participants learn names quickly by association. Gather the group into a circle facing inwards, then tell them that each person will introduce themselves by using their first name preceded by an adjective that starts with the same letter (alliteration), for instance Jumping Julie, Howling Hanif.

   Nominate one person to start off. This person steps into the circle, says their name and steps back. Going clockwise, the next person steps forward, says their name and also the previous name before stepping back. The person following steps forward, says their name and the previous two names, and so on until everyone has stepped into the circle, given their name and all the previous names. This will get harder as the game goes on.

   The game can be adapted so that names are accompanied by parts of the body, for instance Sinita Sinew, or Anne Aorta Artery.

2 **Sharks**

   Gather the group into a circle facing inwards. Hand a sheet of newspaper to each person and tell the group to follow your movements carefully so as not to get lost, then rip your sheet of paper in two, stand on one half, violently screw up the other half and throw it into the middle of the circle.

   You now have a lagoon of shark-infested water and everybody is living on their own little island in the archipelago. This is an ordered society and everybody must live in alphabetical order, so tell the group where A starts and ask them to rearrange themselves by moving from island to island without falling into the shark-infested waters.

   The group must devise an effective way of finding out each other's names – this will probably be quite simply by shouting them out – and moving to their places.

3 **Name graffiti**

   This is for smaller groups. With the group sitting in a circle, place a flipchart sheet and marker pen on the floor and ask everyone to sign their name on it and then tell the group about their name. For instance:

- they like their name;
- they *hate* their name;
- it's short for something else;
- they were named after someone;
- their name means something specific.

4 Zombies

Gather the group into a circle facing inwards, from where they introduce themselves. Now find a volunteer to be the zombie, or Frankenstein's monster, and tell them to walk towards a person in the circle. That person must point out another person in the circle and shout out their name before the zombie gets them. If they shout someone's name in time, the zombie will turn and head for that person. If they don't shout out a name before the zombie gets them, they will become the zombie.

Trust games

1 Sightless walk

Split the group into pairs. One member of each pair elects to close their eyes and keep them tightly shut (or be blindfolded, if the resources are available) and will choose how the other person is to guide them around the room – for instance, with a hand on their shoulder or by holding hands. After five minutes or so, the pairs should swap roles.

2 Concrete mixer

You need groups of at least six and no more than 12 people. One person stands with their feet together, eyes shut and arms folded in the middle of the group who then come together to form a tight circle. The person in the middle falls backwards until they are stopped by a member of the group standing behind, who then gently pushes the person forwards or sideways so that they are caught by someone else. This then turns into a gentle pushing backwards, forwards and around the circle.

The natural reflex for the person in the middle is to put a foot out to stop falling and it takes some self-control to avoid doing this. It works best if the first few catchers are very close to the person in the middle so that they barely start falling before they are caught. This can then develop into a situation where the person in the middle trusts the others so much that they may be flung about quite violently and still believe that they will be caught. However, take care not to let this get out of hand.

3 Huggy bears

This is a good way of getting people to hug each other. It is also useful for splitting the group into a required number at the end. Shout out instructions for people to get together into groups. For instance, 'Huggy Bears Three' means people will hug together in groups of three. 'Huggy Bears Colour of Trousers' means people will hug in one big group everyone who is wearing the same colour trousers. The game should be played at a quick tempo, moving swiftly from one hugging instruction to the next.

4 Sculpting

In groups of three, participants are allocated one of three roles: clay, model and sculptor. The 'sculptor' is blindfolded, the 'model' forms themselves into a position and the 'clay' curls into a heap on the floor. The sculptor must feel the position of the model and try to mould the clay into the same position. Swap roles and repeat.

Getting to know you better games

These games help a group to gel by encouraging each person to say more about themselves. There is the possibility that very personal issues might be raised at this point and it is important to emphasise that any information is confidential to the group.

1 **Your shield**

   Give each group member a sheet of A4 paper. Ask them to draw the shape of a shield and to divide it into four. They will draw or write something which represents:
   - ambition for life, in the top left section;
   - the most positive thing which has ever happened to them, in the top right section;
   - what they hope to be doing in ten years' time, in the bottom left section;
   - what they hope people will say about them after they die, in the bottom right section.

   Ask each member of the group to present their shields and describe what each section means.

2 **Guess who?**

   Prepare a sheet of five to ten questions and hand out a copy to each member of the group. The questions should include things like, 'What was the first CD you ever bought?' or 'What was the most embarrassing moment in your life?' Individuals have ten minutes to fill in the sheet and should not show it to anyone else. All the sheets are collected by the worker then read out at random and the rest of the group has to guess whose sheet it is by the answers given.

   A word of warning. Young people are sometimes a little too honest and it may be worth looking through the sheets first in case any of the stories are too embarrassing to be read out.

3 **Introduce your clothes**

   This is similar to the name graffiti, but in this case everyone is asked to introduce their clothes. They will come up with things like:
   - where they got items from;
   - whether anything is borrowed;
   - whether they like their clothes or not;
   - what their clothes say about them.

Parachute games

These activities are actually run with a parachute, either a real one which has been scrapped and had the rigging taken off, or (more usually) a purpose-made playchute. These are available in rainbow or dayglo colours and the games are particularly good for large groups.

Parachute games are participatory and they involve cooperative work, usually in a circle. The simplest game might be for the members of a group to stand around the rim of the parachute and, by working together, to raise it into a mushroom shape. With 100 young people and a 12-metre playchute, this simple game can be spectacular.

Games can be played on top, underneath or around the chutes, ranging from the maniacally energetic to games that are calming and relaxing. They have uses in educational, leisure and therapeutic settings, and the content of the games can be changed to fit different settings – for instance it is possible to play parachute games as information-gathering exercises on anything from favourite breakfasts to experiences of bullying. (For details about parachute games and training, see page 95.)

exercise 10

Positive appreciation

Aim
To create a bond between members of the group. This exercise is also helpful as an ending exercise for groups who have completed a task.

Group size
Up to 10 people

Materials
Pair of scissors; ball of wool/string

1. Sit the group in a tight circle facing inwards. Start by wrapping the wool around one of your fingers and then pass the ball to someone in the group you wish to thank. For example, you might thank someone for making you laugh a lot that day. The person who has received the wool should then do the same, wrapping some wool around their finger and then passing the ball to someone they wish to thank. If a group member gets stuck, anyone can request the ball of wool and carry on, and this can provide a good opportunity for the worker to ask for the wool and pass it to someone who has not yet received it.

2. At the end of the session, everyone should have some wool wrapped around their finger with what looks like a spider web connecting the group together. Acknowledge the fact that your time on this occasion is at an end and use the scissors to cut the wool linking you together as a group. The group members can then depart with a ring of wool on their finger to remind them of their experience.

Note A:
In any group there may be one or more members who did not gel with the rest. You must be aware of this dynamic when doing this exercise and ensure that these individuals are included.

Note B:
This exercise can be used to close a group entirely, for instance at the very end of a conference or at the disbanding of a committee. On these occasions, the cutting of the wool can be quite an emotional experience for many group members.

exercise 11

Negotiating the ground rules

Aim
To agree on the arrangements for working together.

Group size
Unlimited

Materials
Flipchart/blackboard/large piece of paper, pens/chalk

1 Ask the group to brainstorm what rules they think are needed to enable everybody to feel comfortable about working with and respecting each other. Write all the points raised on the flipchart or blackboard so that everyone can see them. Issues likely to be raised are things like confidentiality, respect for each other's point of view or a change in seating arrangement. If it is a residential event, issues such as being able to drink alcohol while working and times for going to bed are also likely to be raised. Add to the list any issues that have not been raised, but which you feel should be covered.

2 Take each issue raised and allow the group to discuss it until agreement has been reached among the group members and with the workers. Take care to be honest and, if you cannot agree with the group, explain your reasons fully. For instance, your legal obligations will forbid you to allow the consumption of alcohol by anyone under the age of 18, and you may suggest that even those over 18 should not drink.

3 Make it clear that the agreements reached during the discussion will form the basis for all the group's future work. If any of these arrangements is found not to work in practice, it can be changed in the future, by agreement across the whole group.

exercise 12

The ideal worker

Aim
To identify the needs of children or young people in relation to workers' skills, attitudes and qualities. This is a useful exercise for drawing up person specifications and job descriptions for workers.

Group size
Unlimited

Materials
Flipchart/blackboard/large piece of paper, pens/chalk, selected art materials

1. Ask the group to brainstorm the skills, attitudes and qualities they feel are needed for a person to work with them in the context of the setting they are in. Alternatively, ask them to brainstorm their dream worker and nightmare worker. Write all the points raised on the flipchart or blackboard so that everyone can see them. Examples of the perfect worker's qualities may include: is a good listener, has sense of humour and is kind.

2. Go through the list and allow the group to discuss each point.

3. Split the group into smaller groups of three to five people and taking the list of skills, attitudes and qualities attempt through any art means available to produce the ideal worker. For instance, if the children were to draw pictures of the perfect worker described in Part 1 of this exercise, they might draw someone with huge ears (a good listener), a wide grin (sense of humour) and a big pink heart right in the middle of their body (is kind).

   These qualities may also be expressed through papier maché models, junk sculpture or any other artistic media that professionals and young people feel comfortable with and have resources for.

Note:
As a worker, the issues raised in this exercise focus on you and some of the points may be rather personal. Remember always to keep your sense of humour and to take on the points raised and change practice accordingly, wherever possible. It may not be a good idea to use this exercise too early on if the relationship between you and the group is a little uncomfortable.

exercise 13

The Bill of Rights

Aim
To consider the needs of the group in working together.

Group size
Part 1: groups of 3 to 5 people
Parts 2 and 3: unlimited

Materials
A4 sheets of paper for small groups, flipchart/blackboard/large piece of paper, pens/chalk

1 Ask the small groups to brainstorm what rights they feel each individual should have within the group. You can use some of the statements from the Bill of Rights below to give the children an idea of what is intended, or make up your own. Allow about 20 minutes for this.

2 Feed back the discussions to the whole group and negotiate a Bill of Rights that everyone feels comfortable with. Emphasise that, while the rights are expressed in the first person, they apply to all the members of the group and that everybody must acknowledge everyone else's rights.

Example Bill of Rights

(a) I have the right to state my own needs and set my own priorities as a person, independent of any roles that I may assume in my life.

(b) I have the right to be treated with respect as an intelligent, capable and equal human being.

(c) I have the right to express my feelings.

(d) I have the right to express my own opinions and values.

(e) I have the right to say 'yes' and 'no' for myself.

(f) I have the right to make mistakes.

(g) I have the right to change my mind.

(h) I have the right to say I don't understand.

(i) I have the right to ask for what I want.

(j) I have the right to decline responsibility for other people's problems.

(k) I have the right to deal with others without being dependent on them for approval.

(Dickson 1982)

3 Once the Bill of Rights has been created ensure that everyone understands that these individual rights will now apply whenever the group is working together.

exercise 14

Consensus decision-making

Aim
To look at the difference between individual and group decision-making.

Group size
Part 1: individuals
Part 2: up to 10 people

Materials
List of cases, background information and a fine sheet for each group member.

1. The list of cases below, plus background information and a fine sheet are distributed to each member of the group. You can briefly discuss the background information with the group and then individuals have 10-15 minutes to decide on the appropriate fine for each case.

2. The group comes together as a committee and must agree on all the fines through discussion. It is up to the group how they come to agree, but a voting system should be avoided. Encourage the group to view differences of opinion as helpful rather than obstructive, and make it clear that all decisions should be made by consensus. Allow 40 minutes to one hour for this part of the exercise. The group should understand that no more time will be allowed and that they must therefore reach quite a swift consensus on each case. Each group member can write down the committee fine on their own fine sheet, and note the difference between the two.

3. End the session with a discussion about how the committee decisions were reached. You should cover the following points:
   - did anyone chair the meeting?
   - was the discussion dominated by a few voices?
   - did anyone remain passive?
   - did the group really reach a consensus?
   - was lack of time a problem towards the end?
   - what issues did they consider when setting the fines?
   - were the individual fines generally more lenient than the committee fines, or was it the other way around?

Background information

Under the 1995 Reform of the Justice for Children and Young People Act, people found guilty of a crime against the UN Convention of the Rights of the Child can be fined. A committee of magistrates is considering ten cases and agreeing fines for each. In all the cases, the people have been found guilty. You are provided with a brief description of the circumstances surrounding the case and are told whether or not the person(s) involved pleaded guilty or not guilty to the charge.

The committee can award fines of between £50 to £5,000, in multiples of £10.

The cases:

A   A school failed to allow a 12-year-old girl the right to be heard before expulsion. The school pleaded guilty to contravening section 12 of the Act.

B   The father of an 11-year-old boy resorted to corporal punishment using a walking stick after a dispute over bedtimes. The father pleaded not guilty to the offence but was convicted under section 19 of the Act.

C   A local authority announced the closure of a children's residential unit prior to the completion of consultation with young residents. The authority pleaded guilty to contravening section 12 of the Act.

D   The UK government failed to consult widely with other organisations on its report for implementing the UN Convention after it allowed only eight days over Christmas for them to submit their views. The government pleaded not guilty of contravening section 43(iii) of the Act.

E   A school which expelled a 14-year-old girl for attempting to set up a campaign group on animal rights pleaded guilty to contravening the rights of young people to freedom of assembly as laid out in section 15 of the Act.

F   A residential social worker who opened the correspondence of a nine-year-old girl claiming that he felt it may have been from a past abuser was found guilty of infringing her right to privacy, under section 16 of the Act.

G   A mother who broke her 15-year-old daughter's nose after finding her smoking pleaded not guilty, claiming it was in her daughter's best interests. She was found guilty of contravening section 19 of the Act.

H   A local authority passed planning permission for a new road without consulting the children's forum. The authority pleaded guilty of contravening Article 12 of the Act.

I   The parents of a 12-year-old girl were found guilty of contravening the right to freedom of conscience under section 14 of the Act after attempting to force feed their daughter meat on the grounds that they did not feel a vegan diet was healthy.

J   Foster parents of an 11-year-old boy pleaded guilty to contravening his right to appropriate information under section 17 of the Act after refusing to allow him to attend school during a day on sex education.

The fine sheet

	Individual fine	Committee fine	Difference
Case A			
Case B			
Case C			
Case D			
Case E			
Case F			
Case G			
Case H			
Case I			
Case J			
Total difference			

5 Initial involvement

There is a tendency among professionals to expect more from the involvement of children and young people than they would from involving any other group. The most common concern is whether the consulted group is truly representative and not just an elite few.

Representative groups of children are no different from those in any other user group; they can speak legitimately for larger groups when discussing issues of specific concern to that larger group and will often do so through their own process of consultation. They should not be expected to represent the exact views of every member in the larger group, and will speak instead for a cross-section of those views. Nor should a representative group be immediately rejected if it does not precisely reflect the gender or cultural balance of the larger group. Care must be taken on these issues, but genuine enthusiasm may count for more.

There is also a danger in expecting too much commitment from young people. There will usually be peaks and troughs in the level of their support for a particular initiative. It is up to professionals to provide ongoing training and new input which will hold young people's interest.

Consideration should also be given to the fact that a group of children or young people may not reach the conclusion on a given issue that professionals either expect or hope for.

Providing children with essential information

From the outset, those children being consulted should be given as much information as possible and dialogue should be open and honest. Professionals must be up-front about what young people can really expect from the experience and it is essential to be clear about what can and what cannot be changed, who will be setting the agenda, any opposition to empowerment within the organisation, and how far any individual can expect to be involved.

If appropriate, it may be helpful to go through **Exercise 1** (page 9) with the young people and to discuss the organisation's views regarding each of the questions. This is also a good time to adapt that exercise for young people and to elicit their views (for instance, Question 1 might become 'What do you hope to achieve through your involvement in decision-making?').

It is important at this stage to discuss the different agendas which children and professionals may be working to. By bringing them out in the open, the potential for future misunderstanding is considerably reduced.

Checklist 5 lists the basics for preparing the ground for a meeting, conference or other consultation. Any organisation interested in participation should generate a more specific checklist to cover its own context. For instance in *Child Health Rights* (BACCH/CRO 1995), it is suggested that health providers should:

- 'Employ people who are skilled in communicating with children and young people of different ages;
- Make sure the child or young person has as much information about their medical condition as they want;
- Give clear information about treatments and how effective they are likely to be – discussing disadvantages as well as benefits;

Checklist 5

Preparing the ground for a meeting, conference or other consultation

1 Prior to a meeting, young people should have:
   - clear and accessible details about the aim of the meeting
   - an understanding of their role at the meeting
   - a copy of the agenda
   - information about other people who will be attending
   - a chance to pre-meet
   - an understanding of the level of their involvement
   - a reminder of the meeting close to the event

2 The following issues should have been considered in order to make the meeting accessible to children:
   - time and date of the meeting
   - transport to and from the venue
   - formality of the venue
   - the layout of the room
   - preparation of icebreaker exercises
   - expenses for the children
   - type of language used by professionals (especially in relation to jargon)

3 Issues for consideration when planning a conference:
   - have the children been given adequate time and resources to prepare?
   - have the young people been given an opportunity to experiment with different media for presentation and review, such as drama, art, video or using tape recordings?

4 Children and young people who are being asked to take part in research must be given enough time to think it over and must have given their personal consent to it. The following information should be provided in full prior to undertaking the work:
   - purpose of the research and what it hopes to achieve
   - explanation of how the research will be done, e.g. by interview, diary, or case study
   - media to be used in collecting information, e.g. audio tape, video, or film
   - if the research is to involve comparison, explanation of how the different test groups will work
   - duration of whole research and of specific interviews
   - venue for research interviews
   - number of people to be involved
   - whether or not a parent or friend can sit in while the research is being undertaken
   - voluntary nature of participation – no participant should feel obliged to answer any questions
   - whether identity of participants is to be confidential or published, and how the relevant case will be achieved
   - details of claimable expenses and how they are to be supplied
   - details of any rewards which may be forthcoming to the participants

- Give information on the side-effects of treatment and the mode of administration of drugs;
- Seek child's involvement in monitoring therapy;
- Give information on immunisation;
- Consult the child on school issues such as medication;
- Give information on access to medical records.'

Who to consult, and how

If a group of young people is to speak for a larger group, some method of choosing the representative group must be found. This is quite simple if the target group is small and specific, for instance if a youth club wishes to consult its membership about its constitution. However, the situation is not so clear-cut for a local authority wishing to consult children and young people in its area. A consultation may have to cover children and young people aged between 0 and 18 years, and the needs of service users would differ hugely – even more so because individuals within the group will be living in very different environments. Under these circumstances, the authority's best solution would not be to form a new group for the purposes of consultation, but to look within the community of children and find an existing group which meets on a regular basis and which is accustomed to discussing issues. A local 'in-care group' would, therefore, be the conduit through which to discuss, say, after-care arrangements, while youth clubs or youth councils would be consulted about more general services in the area.

Once the representative group has been identified, early consultations should allow both young people and professionals to identify the key areas of an ongoing consultation. There are two basic methods for gathering this information. Quantitative methodology makes use of devices such as questionnaires to find out views on particular issues, and qualitative methodology involves group discussion.

Questionnaires are most useful when canvassing the views of a large number of people, but by their very nature they limit the views that can be expressed and should only be used as background information to group discussion. Questionnaires which invite opinion through open-ended questions (see Figure 5.1) tend to provide more useful information than those which demand fixed answers and box-ticking (see Figure 5.2). Even so, the randomness of responses generated by open-ended questionnaires makes them difficult to process, and if those responses are highly diverse it may become impossible to detect a solid trend in views.

While questionnaires may produce some background, the real productive work must be done through the qualitative methodology of group discussion. **Exercises 15 to 17** (pages 61 to 65) show some ways of encouraging young people to express their views and initiate meaningful discussion. They generally make use of qualitative methodology, though **Exercise 15** does include an example of a questionnaire.

Figure 5.1

Example of open-ended questions questionnaire

MANCHESTER CITY COUNCIL

Views of children and young people

Please answer the questions below by yourself or with some friends to help Manchester City Council find out what children and young people like to do in their free time.

How old are you?

Are you a girl or a boy?

What part of Manchester do you live in?

What do you do with most of your free time outside school:

i) in the evenings?

ii) at weekends?

iii) in the school holidays?

What do you like to do for fun?

What stops you from doing what you want to do?

What do you like to do when you have money to spend?

What things would you like in your area to make things less boring when you don't have any money to spend?

Thanks for helping us today.

Figure 5.2

Example of box-tick questionnaire

YOUR FREE TIME (from school)

Do you enjoy it?
Or could it be better?

> The City Council is trying to find out what children and young people (from about 8 – 14 yrs old) most like to do in the evenings, at weekends and in the school holidays.
>
> *Please help us* by filling in this form and either:
> (a)   give it to your teacher, playworker or club leader to send back to us, or
> (b)   post it to us

Your name –

Your school –

Your age –

What do you do now in your *free time*? Please tick the boxes which describe the things you do in your free time.

Watch television	☐	Watch videos	☐
Play music	☐	Play computer games	☐
Do homework	☐	Laze around	☐
Look after brothers and sisters	☐	Go to the shops	☐
Meet your friends *your* house	☐	Meet your friends *their* house	☐
Meet your friends outside	☐	Meet your friends in the park	☐
Meet your friends on the playground	☐	Meet your friends somewhere else	☐ (Please say where)...
Play football	☐	Play rounders	☐
Play another sport	☐	(Please say which)..	
Go swimming	☐	Go to the pictures	☐
Go to Laser Quest	☐	Go to a club	☐ (Please say what sort of club)...............................
Have 'extra' lessons	☐	(Please say what)...	
Do jobs for your Mum and Dad	☐	Do a paper round	☐
Do another job or jobs	☐	(Please say what)..	
Anything else, eg hobbies?	☐	(Please tell us)..	

What would you like to do more of if you could (*please list below*)?

What stops you from doing the things you like in your free time (*please list below*)?

Taking action

Consultation is not, of course, an end in itself. Once information has been gathered and views expressed, action needs to be considered along the lines suggested by group discussion. **Exercise 17** looks at prioritising issues and drawing up an action plan which can lead directly to action being taken. The following example of an action plan was drawn up by UNICEF (Fountain 1993) to help young people around the world promote the UN Convention on the Rights of the Child. It is written in the imperative and is basically a 'To Do' list. It shows how far-reaching action planning can be.

Action to take on a local level:
- Find out about the services for children and young people in your area. Does every child have equal access to education? Health care? Recreation facilities?
- Volunteer to work or fundraise for a local organisation that provides services to children.
- Take part in local action, such as environment clean-up days, cultural festivals, building playground equipment etc.
- Write letters to the editor of the local newspaper to express your ideas on children's rights.
- Lobby local councillors to provide better services for children and families in your area.

Action to take on a national level:
- Find out if your government has signed/ratified the Convention on the Rights of the Child.
- Find out who in your government has responsibility for seeing that the Convention is implemented, and whether any changes in the law, in social services and/or in education services have been brought about in your country.
- If there is a UNICEF office of National Committee in your country, contact them to find out how you can participate in the promotion of children's rights.
- Write to your local elected representative if you feel that more could be done to implement the Convention in your country.
- Make the Convention a live political issue. Before elections, ask candidates for political office what they intend to do about implementing it. Get the Convention put on to party platforms.

Action to take on a global level:
- Find out about places in your part of the world and in other countries where children's rights are infringed.
- Join an international human rights organisation. Campaign or fundraise for it.
- Use your role as a consumer to express your opinions. Avoid buying products from companies that use child labour, pollute the environment, discriminate against minorities, etc.
- Lobby your representatives in international organisations (the United Nations, the European Union, the Organization of American States, etc.) to draw attention to the infringement of children's rights. Give them your support for action on children's rights.

(UNICEF 1993)

exercise 15

What do you really think?

Aim
To provide children and young people with an opportunity to explore their own attitudes, and to begin discussing them openly.

Group size
Unlimited

Materials
Version 1: A room with space to run in; four A3 pieces of paper
Version 2: Copies of written questionnaires plus pens/pencils

Version 1

1. Make four signs on A3 paper which say 'Agree', 'Disagree', 'Strongly agree', and 'Strongly disagree', or which express these views with symbols/artwork. For instance, 'Agree' might be represented by a medium-sized black tick and 'Strongly agree' by a huge red tick, with crosses for the disagrees. For younger children you could use smiley faces and angry faces. Put each sign in a corner of the room.

2. Read out a prepared statement which has relevance to the group and then ask the participants to run or walk to the corner which most closely represents their response to the statement. For instance, a group of young people may be infuriated by the statement: 'Groups of young people should not hang around the shopping centre having a good time', in which case a number of them they would go to the 'Strongly disagree' corner.

3. After each occasion, the group is brought back to the centre where they have a short discussion about their views and about why some will disagree with a statement while others disagree. Following the discussion, participants should then go back into the corners to see if anyone has changed their mind. Another statement is then read and the process repeated.

    The following examples indicate the sort of contentious issues that can be broached in this exercise, though the exercise will only work if the statements have clear relevance to the participants' context.

    (a) If the parents agree, childminders should be allowed to smack children in their care.
    (b) Local Authorities should close down nurseries/playgroups that do not have sufficient books and resources covering race, such as black dolls and multi-racial books.
    (c) In cases of divorce and separation, children should determine who has legal custody of them.
    (d) Babies should decide when they want to feed themselves, not every four hours as determined by professionals.
    (e) The voting age should be the same as the age of criminal responsibility, that is ten in England and Wales, and eight in Scotland.
    (f) In Finland it is against the law to make important family decisions without consulting your children. It should be the same in the UK.

Version 2

1. Each member of the group is given a printed questionnaire which asks the same kind of questions as those suggested above. Without conferring, individuals fill in the questionnaire by ticking the box which most closely reflects their response to each statement, then the questionnaires are collected in.

2. The responses are counted and the group then discusses reasons why there might be general concurrence on certain issues, while others may display more polarised views.

    Here is an example of a questionnaire that appeared in *Participation – Youth Work Curriculum Guidelines* (YCNI 1993). It looks at styles of leadership in a youth club and shows the sorts of questions that relate to a specific context. These could be used in either version of the exercise.

	Strongly agree	Agree	Disagree	Strongly disagree
Adult leaders can organise and run things better and more quickly than young people.				
The club should be well run, with lots of activities.				
The club has always been run / managed / organised in the same way.				
Everyone is happy with the way things are run.				
Young people know adult leaders are in charge and they show adults respect.				
The members want the programme given to them by the adult leaders.				
Routine and order make for a well-run club.				
Everyone must be sensible and logical about problems in the club.				
The adult leaders have lots of experience and the necessary information about organising the club, so members like it when the leaders tell them what the club will provide.				

exercise 16

Exploring the issues

Aim
To quickly generate a pool of ideas and then to prioritise the issues raised.

Group size
Part 1: groups of 6 to 16 people
Part 2: individuals or pairs
Part 3: gradually grows into the whole group

Materials
Flipchart, pens, paper, filing cards

1. Brainstorm ideas that will highlight specific issues or identify jobs to be done through forthcoming participation. The main purpose of this part of the brainstorm is for children to contribute their views by shouting out whatever comes to mind that is relevant to the subject. Encourage imagination and accept all the points being offered, however unlikely they may seem. Discourage discussion at this point (that will come later), though do give young people time to elaborate on their individual points.

   As an example, the following suggestions were offered by a group of eight- to 12-year-olds who were consulted in Manchester through play groups and junior youth councils. They were asked what was wrong with the area they lived in and came up with:

Being run over	Burglars	Pollution
Drunks	Dog poo	Criminals
Rubbish	Bad people	Cops
Drugs	Fighting	Getting robbed
Smoke	Graffiti	House robbed
Killing people	Dirty	Living on the street

   For younger children, you could replace brainstorming with a storyboard. Using the Manchester example, children might be asked to draw a picture of their street with all the things they do not like shown on it, or the group could make a collective picture, in which each child draws a picture of the thing they dislike most and then all the pictures are displayed together.

2. For every participant each point is written on a separate card, with any that double up merged on to one card (for instance, Bad People and Criminals in the list above might be combined, unless they are specified as completely different things). Each individual or pair then decides on a priority of issues by arranging the cards into a diamond shape. They must choose a single issue as the most important (this will form the top of the diamond) and a single issue as the least important (the bottom of the diamond). Within those two extremes, there will be several mid-ranking issues. For instance, in Manchester one of the young people might have come up with:

63 Working with children and young people

                    Getting robbed
         Pollution   Living on the street
  Being run over   Fighting   Criminals
         Graffiti   Dog poo
                      Rubbish

3 Once individuals have completed this, they double up with another individual and must decide on their preferred diamond ranking. In most cases the individual rankings will differ in some way, and so the two must negotiate a new joint diamond. Give them a limited amount of time in which to do this (5-10 minutes), then double up the pairs into fours and ask them to negotiate a new diamond. Continue doubling up and negotiating until finally the whole group comes together to reach a consensus.

exercise 17

Action planning

Aim
To encourage young people to think of a variety of ways in which they might take action on given issues.

Group size
Unlimited

Materials
Flipchart and pens, or blackboard and chalk

This exercise follows on from Exercise 16, or from any other exercise in which children have identified and prioritised the issues that most concern them.

1. Ask the group to brainstorm ideas for dealing with the highest priority issue. Again, all suggestions should be taken.

2. Once all suggestions are displayed, the group will then quickly review them and discard any that appear unlikely to work. The group should then debate any difficulties that might be encountered in carrying out the suggestions which remain. For instance, if the young people in Manchester were looking to solve their problem of getting robbed, one of their suggestions could be to form a young people's surveillance group. The potential problems here might be:
   - a lot of young people will have to give up a lot of their time to make it work;
   - the rest of the community may be against the surveillance group;
   - the surveillance group could become over zealous and start using vigilante tactics.

   For each suggestion, the group must decide whether the potential difficulties would rule out the project, or whether there might be ways to overcome them.

3. The group should then try to reduce the list of action projects to a manageable length. They should be convinced that all the points listed are genuinely possible and could run alongside one another. You may wish to evaluate the final list in more depth with the group and settle on just one or two courses of action, or even suggest that smaller groups could work on different projects.

4. Take action. Go ahead with the projects that were agreed upon.

part 3
long-term involvement

6 Developing policy and practice

There are no exercises linked with this chapter because once organisations reach the level of long-term involvement, the need for exercises in confidence-building should have passed. Instead, this chapter examines the requirements for long-term involvement, looks at the key issue of developing a policy for consultation and offers several examples of successful involvement.

Handing over power

The long-term involvement of children and young people can take many different forms and depends on the level to which an organisation wishes to hand over power and responsibility. Young people may be involved through:

- being members of a management board;
- planning conferences from start to finish;
- interviewing staff;
- being members of an ongoing local children's forum;
- seeing a long-term consultation through to eventual policy change.

Children and young people who are invited to contribute may not be automatically grateful for the 'wonderful opportunity' they have been given. The methods of involvement and structure of the organisation itself may come under justifiable criticism, and if consultation is to mean anything these grievances must be taken seriously. However, giving up power need not be as worrying as it sounds. If children and young people are provided with detailed information they can, in some circumstances, serve an organisation better than its adult professionals. For instance, children and young people may be more efficient at designing and organising publicity for a project which aims to serve their peers because they know from first-hand experience what is likely to attract them.

Figure 6.1 is an example of what can be achieved by this kind of involvement. Poster (a) was put together by the adult professionals who ran Off the Record and who wanted to use simple, direct language to describe the service accurately and give a clear explanation which would be accessible to their target audience.

Not long after the poster campaign, staff at Off the Record began a series of consultations with young people and discovered that their posters had confused their target audience rather than enlightening them. It was therefore decided to relaunch the poster campaign using ideas which had been suggested by the young people, and poster (b) was the result. The cartoons immediately jump out of this second poster, making a trip to Off the Record look far more inviting. However, the real innovation lay in the words around the edge of the poster. During consultation, professionals discovered that young people reading their posters did not understand what was being offered. The words 'Information', 'Advice' and 'Counselling' were both vague and a little daunting, and young people were not sure whether or not the centre would serve their personal needs. By adding the words 'Pregnancy', 'Homelessness', 'Welfare Benefits' etc., poster (b) made it clear to everyone that the information, advice and counselling could relate to those specific needs.

Figure 6.1

Poster (a)

Poster (b)

Off the Record benefited considerably from this new campaign, as did the young people involved and also those who needed to use the service. This kind of consultation might also be effective in more controversial areas such as promoting safer sex or providing drug education, both areas in which professionals have struggled to provide children and young people with a message that takes account of youth culture.

The Lifechance case study demonstrates a different way of devolving power. In this case, the responsibility for recruiting new staff is shared between young people and professionals. There is flexibility built into the system to allow for different situations, and it is particularly worth noting the key points at the end, in which the author offers advice to other organisations wishing to introduce a similar system.

case study

Involving children and young people in interviewing staff

Lifechance works with disadvantaged young people, including the homeless, single parents, those from ethnic minorities and those with disabilities. On a day-to-day basis the project aims to provide practical support and encouragement. In the longer term it aims to empower young people so that they can participate more effectively in the decisions that effect their lives. Here, Kieran Breen describes how Lifechance goes about involving young people in recruiting its staff.

The Lifechance Project is firmly committed to the principle of involving young people in staff interviews. What follows is a brief outline of how we go about involving young people.

- Equal opportunities applied.

1 All Lifechance recruitment and interview procedures take place within an equal opportunities framework. Hence each job description has a clear person specification.

- Role of young people made clear.

2 The project decides which bits of the person specification young people are qualified to interview on. This is normally sections covering 'ability to relate to young people', or 'awareness of issues facing young people'.

- Representation thought out.

3 The project then decides how many young people will be involved and attempts to get a representative cross-section of the young people, e.g. by gender and race. We allow the young people we work with to ultimately decide who will be on the panel. NOTE: Depending on the job, some candidates are interviewed by a joint panel of workers and young people – others by separate panels of workers and young people.

- Level of responsibility made clear.

4 The project is clear with young people about the extent of their role (for instance, although there are nine person specifications, the young people may only be judging on two of them) and how they must operate within our project's equal opportunities framework.

- Power-sharing alternative.

5 After interviews are completed, young people's opinions are aggregated into overall scores and the top candidate is appointed. It may be that the young people's favourite candidate is not appointed, though the panel may decide that if the young people fail a candidate, then that person cannot be appointed.

Key points to be aware of about involving young people in recruitment:
- Be clear with young people about the range and extent of their role.
- Having been clear, let them get on with it – don't tell them what to ask.
- Look at how person specifications are framed – decide which areas young people can judge.
- Be prepared to question your own assumptions and interview procedures.

Developing a policy for involvement

In the long term, it is vital that the processes which empower children and young people can not simply be dropped if the personnel within an organisation changes. Where children and young people have been involved in decision-making, this process should be incorporated into the organisation's constitution and institutionalised in everything it does.

An essential springboard for doing this is to formalise a policy, and any policy must be developed in relation to the 12 key questions which were asked in Exercise 1:

1 What are you aiming to achieve by empowering the children and young people you work with?
2 Where are you in relation to that aim?
3 What will the children and young people get out of it?
4 Are you prepared for the resource implications?
5 Why have you not done it before?
6 Are you prepared to involve children and young people from the start?

7 Are you being honest with the children and young people?
8 What are your expectations?
9 Are you prepared to give up some power?
10 Are you prepared to take some criticism?
11 Do you recognise this as a long-term commitment?
12 Are you prepared to institutionalise the change?

The policy statement should arise from discussions with professionals at all levels within the organisation – so that everyone feels they are part of it – and also with the children, without whose contribution the policy could have no credibility. An agreed initial statement of aims should not be seen as a substitute for action, but should create a framework for development and a timetable for action. The policy document must:
- state its aims and perceived benefits;
- show how it will link with other documents and build on them, such as the organisation's equal opportunities policy or the UN Convention on the Rights of the Child;
- address specific objectives towards developing the empowerment of groups and individuals;
- identify the barriers within the organisation and show how they will be overcome;
- identify the staff, training and financial resources needed to implement the policy;
- explain methods for monitoring and evaluating the policy's progress;
- identify the role/person responsible for coordinating the policy.

This last point is critical. The policy coordinator is the conduit for communication between the professionals and the children. This person will be responsible for providing young people with good information, training special workers and the young people themselves, and will also have to provide the organisation with progress reports. The worker who takes on this role must therefore have a strong connection with the children while also being in accord with the organisation's general aims and objectives.

Success

The final case study is a description of a Merseyside project which successfully involved local children and young people, and which continues to do so. The case study has been given in detail to show each step that was taken so that readers can see how a long-term programme of involvement develops and grows. It also provides information on the kind of problems which can occur in this sort of project.

case study

The Children's Council in the West Everton Community Council area

- Initial consultation with children. Children raise own agenda.

- Issues fed into community. Response leads to formal Children's Council.

In October 1990, the West Everton Community Council held a meeting at which concern was expressed about the lack of facilities for children in the Council's area. The nearby Mansfield Youth Club had been closed down and the Salisbury Club demolished to make way for new housing. Drugs presented a major problem, stolen cars were being driven at high speed throughout the area and it was simply not safe for children to be out on the street.

These problems and suggested solutions were referred to the wider network of neighbourhood groups in West Everton for discussion and were included on the agenda for the WECC Steering Group. Feedback from these groups showed that there were pockets of children from each of the eight areas covered who were reluctant to cross each other's boundaries. The aim, then, was to break that inhibition, to provide children with adequate play facilities, to ensure that all children would feel able to use them wherever they were, and to devise a system in which children could express themselves and have some input in making

- Brainstorm ideas and prioritise issues.

- Children take responsibility for an event.

- Children evaluate and develop idea of Children's Council.

- Adult support secured.

- Council tackles issues relevant to local children.

- Children begin to look at community issues.

- Eventual decline of Council.

decisions which would affect their lives. Workers from WECC and a representative from Liverpool City Council met with parents and others to find a way of achieving all these aims, and the idea of a Children's Council began to emerge.

A special meeting for all children across the area was attended by more than 100 children and young people in February 1992 and their enthusiasm was clear. The organisers broke them up into groups determined by the distinct area in which they lived and asked them to say what was GOOD and what was BAD about their district. They were also asked for suggestions for change across the whole community and, using a flipchart, were invited to prioritise the ideas they came up with.

To build on this event and to show community involvement was not all about meetings, the first task was for the children to organise and run their own disco. It was held just ten days after the first meeting and the children did all the work – with the support of parents and community workers – including booking the hall and disco, arranging the food and cleaning up afterwards. The event was a huge success and, afterwards, the children involved in organising the event sent thank you letters to everyone who had helped. In those letters, they asked for more activities.

A feedback meeting with the children was arranged for a week later to look at the pros and cons of the event. Other issues came up, such as road safety, green issues, the children's concern for older people and the lack of facilities for children right across the area. The seed for an ongoing Children's Council to look into these issues was beginning to take root, though it was not all plain sailing. Some of the children began to drop out and the remainder realised that it was not so easy to make arrangements for activities involving large numbers of their peers. Smaller meetings were therefore arranged by and for the children, with individual children rotating as chair and secretary for each one.

At this point, Save the Children became interested in this growing programme of consultation and offered to fund a Children's Worker for the Everton area. The idea was instantly supported by the children and an appointment made in early 1993. The 'Kids' Council' (as the children preferred to call it) started monthly meetings which continued until 1994. Every child in the area was a member – even if they were only two years old, *they* could decide what colour they wanted their jelly to be.

The project develops

Most of the Kids' Council's early activity took place in the southern end of the patch – Langsdale and Islington – as this was where the lack of facilities was most acute. The area and its housing was appalling, with half the houses and maisonettes either vacated or vandalised. As part of the area's housing was being developed under the Vacant Stock Initiative, the Kids' Council contacted the Tenants' Group and asked for sleeping policemen to be included in the plans. The Tenants' Group took this up with the Housing Association and sleeping policemen were built as part of the new housing development in late 1993.

The children continued to meet during 1993, albeit in smaller numbers, and they again expressed concern for their parents, grandparents and older people in general. It was decided to start Bingo sessions each Sunday afternoon and they were attended by 30-40 people every week. The children also asked for drama lessons and the Yellow House Drama Group in Bootle came to work with them for six sessions. They helped quieter children express themselves in a positive way and gave everyone a lot of fun as well as experience of the self-discipline needed to perform.

It would be wrong to give the impression that setting up and running the council was easy. In fact, it came to an end in 1994 for several reasons. The resource time available in terms of staff was not adequate for what was very labour-intensive work. Children became disheartened because they felt they were not listened to by some adults outside the project, who refused to take it seriously. More significantly, after the death of an adult volunteer who had been a key figure in motivating the Children's Council, the group fragmented and lost its direction.

Although it no longer functions, for the period it lasted the council provided the children and the entire community with a number of significant benefits. The adults involved in the project learned a lot, and continue to use similar methods in order to make children's voices heard and to bring benefits to local children.

One of the main points to note from the Merseyside case study is that, when the council was working effectively, it constantly evaluated its position by asking its members which projects interested them to ensure that it still served its membership. Some kind of constant re-evaluation is essential so that an organisation keeps up to date with the children it works with, and it is advisable that at least some of this feedback is obtained in writing.

Here are two examples of forms given to children which helped them provide written evaluation. Figure 6.2 asked children for their evaluation of the Children's Society Talgarth Playscheme. Figure 6.3 is an evaluation form used by Essex Children's Rights Service to find out what children thought of an awayday. Both examples use different kinds of faces as their method of evaluation. Figure 6.3 also uses a clock face and other pictures to help children remember specific events on which they are being asked to comment.

Figure 6.2

WHAT I ENJOYED: Talgarth Playscheme

FUN FACTOR

7-11 years

FUN   OK   NO FUN

ART & CRAFT

- Decorated pencil tins
- Collage
- Junk modelling
- Salt & starch models
- Painting eggs

ACTIVITIES

- Roller booting
- Games
- Drama
- Easter egg hunt
- Magic with wizard monkey

TRIPS

- Rhayader Leisure Centre
- Sawmills Gunsmoke

OTHERS

Figure 6.3

GET THE RIGHTS IDEA AWAY DAY

? Please ✓ = ☺ ✓

1. Did you enjoy the away day?
2. Was it a good idea to meet and talk?
3. What did you think of the meeting place?
4. What did you think of the food?
5. Did you enjoy the game we played?
6. What did you think of the guest speaker in the morning?
7. What did you think of the guest speakers in the afternoon?
8. What workshop did you go to in the morning? ✓ What did you think of it?
9. What workshop did you go to in the afternoon? ✓ What did you think of it?
10. Would you come to another day like this?

Thank you for filling in this form. ☺ ✓

74 **Empowering** children and young people

7 Examples of good practice

This final chapter provides outline details for several national and international projects which have sought to empower children and young people through participation. These cases do not seek to provide step-by-step information, but show a range of consultation projects which have worked in practice, giving details about real achievements and the main problems encountered.

1 An article by young people with disabilities in The Children's Society publication, *Children in Focus*

Location:
Children With Disabilities, York.

Start date:
August 1995.

Finish date:
June 1996.

Source of funding:
The Children's Society.

Number and type of staff:
Two PACT project workers, plus support from project administrative staff.

Number and ages of children and young people:
Ten young people, aged 14-24.

Target group:
Young people with disabilities who are, or have been, involved with the PACT Project. (PACT is a Children's Society project which arranges family-based short-term care for children and young people with physical and learning disabilities. Volunteer families provide the care and, in this way, the children and young people experience new relationships and social interaction within a different family environment. PACT regularly consults the children and young people involved with its work to ensure that it is properly serving the needs of young people with disabilities and to provide them with an opportunity to express their views.)

Role of adults:
To facilitate group discussion and provide practical support, e.g. transport and booking rooms.

Aims of project/service provided:
1 To choose a topic about which the group wishes to comment.
2 To devise a format for the group's views.
3 To record the group's expressed views.
4 To publish an article entitled 'People Who Listen and People Who Don't Listen' in The Children's Society magazine, *Children in Focus*.

Outcomes/benefits for children and young people:
The young people involved valued the experience of being part of the group. More specifically, it was an opportunity to present their views in published form and to influence people who read the article.

Problems encountered:
The broad age range and difference in ability within the group made it difficult to manage. Also, the design of the published article differed significantly from what the young people had envisaged.

Main findings of monitoring/research:
1 Discussions need to be pitched at appropriate levels, structured in appropriate ways and held in appropriate venues. Young people must be given time to form and express their views.
2 Care should be taken to allow young people to express their own views and not be influenced by others. It is also important to verify views with the young people at a later date.
3 Including magazine designers and editors in discussions with young people at an early stage will improve communication and help to prevent differences between the young people's views about how the article should look and its actual appearance.

Publications/existing documentation:
The article in question was published in *Children in Focus* in June 1996.

2 Action with Young Carers

Location:
Barnardo's, Liverpool.

Start date:
February 1993.

Number and type of staff:
Two Action with Young Carers workers.

Number and ages of children and young people:
Five female carers aged 12, 13 and 14 (x3).

Target group:
Young female carers who were already involved with Action with Young Carers, Liverpool (the organisation supports and consults with 49 young carers aged 0-18 years in Liverpool). This group of five female carers took on the specific project of talking about the Carers National leaflet.

Role of adults:
Group facilitators/co-ordinators.

Other agencies involved:
None in this specific group.

Aims of project/service provided:
1 *Specific aim for this project:*
- to assist Carers National Association in drafting a leaflet for under-18s about new entitlements available under the Carers Recognition Act. (Carers National had asked for input regarding the sort of information which young carers felt they needed. The young women involved were asked to comment on the first draft produced by Carers National, and then to do the same with the second draft which had been prepared using feedback from young carers across the country.)

2 *General aims for this project:*
- to provide an opportunity specifically for young female carers of about the same age to meet fortnightly and to offer mutual support;
- to provide the female carers with a chance to express views and to plan activities;
- to give them a break from caring (respite, fun and time out from their situation).

Outcomes/benefits for children and young people:
1 *Outcomes:* The group made a number of comments regarding the initial draft of the leaflet. Their recommendations and observations were taken into account and incorporated into the final draft which was then printed and circulated nationally.

2 *Benefits:*
- the young carers provided input for a national leaflet knowing it may help other young women in a similar situation;
- they were given an opportunity to express their views and had concrete evidence in the form of the leaflet that these views were valued and acted upon ('Brilliant,' they said, when they saw that their ideas had been taken on).

Problems encountered:
The main difficulty to overcome was the young carers' lack of confidence and their belief that no one would listen to them. Initial motivation was therefore a problem as the carers did not recognise that they had a voice which could make some change with regards to legislation.

3 Butterflies – Programme of Street and Working Children

Location:
Delhi, India.

Start date:
January 1988.

Source of funding:
Mesreor.

Number and type of staff:
25 staff: 1 director, 10 street educators, 3 health workers, 3 community workers, 1 vocational trainer, 1 researcher, 2 documentation workers, 1 information officer, 3 administrators.

Number and ages of children and young people:
The Butterflies team of street educators are in contact with 800 street and working children, aged 5-18 years.

Target group:
Children and young people who live and/or work in the unitary territory of Delhi (India). Street educators meet the children on the streets in eight areas ('contact points') of Delhi where there is a concentration of street and working children. Special emphasis on the girl child.

Role of adults:
Director: project management, networking, awareness-raising, campaigning, advocacy and documentation; *Street educators:* establish contact with street children and build relationships based on equity and respect. Aim to empower street children (see below) and provide support services; *Mobile health team:* provide preventative approach to health; *Community workers:* community organisation and promotion of child education in one slum area; *Vocational trainer:* development of vocational opportunities; *Researcher and documentors:* research and documentation on unrecognised and unexplored dimensions of child abuse, exploitation and neglect; *Information officer:* quarterly publication of child file, *My Name is Today*; *Administrators:* administrative duties.

Aims of project/service provided:
1 *Main objectives:*
- To empower street children with the knowledge and skills necessary to protest their rights as children and provide them with support and assistance for reinstatement in their families where possible and help them develop as respected and productive citizens.
- To use the UN Convention on the Rights of the Child as a major tool for ensuring government and public accountability to the well-being of all vulnerable children.

2 *Specific objectives include:*
- organise support services (non-formal education; health care; recreation; saving schemes);
- help and protect from worse excesses of exploitation;
- organise children for collective action (cooperatives, credit union, Child Workers' Trade Union);
- provide counselling;
- provide facilities for skill requisition and vocational training;
- raise public awareness and promote social mobilisation activities on issues of exploitation and abuse (e.g. protest rallies and legal action).

3 *Service provided:* Aiming to install the principles of democracy and participation in decision-making, the formation of Children's Councils

(Bal Sabha) has been central to the way of working. Once a month, children from the different contact points come together for a council meeting. Between 50 and 80 children aged 5-18 years usually attend the meeting, where they discuss matters that are important to them, critique ongoing activities and plan future activities. The children and young people elect their own chairperson and also one of the literate children to record minutes and decisions.

Outcomes/benefits for children and young people:

The Children's Council forms the core of the Butterflies programme. It enables the children to organise themselves for collective action and creates a forum where they can speak, share ideas and critique the orientation of the programme. The children and young people also learn the principles of democracy and community participation in decision-making. The Children's Council provides a true child-centred mechanism allowing children's participation in decision-making to be a guiding force in programme orientation. It has resulted in creative child-initiated interventions. For example, Council meetings have resulted in: the children starting their own restaurant (run since 1990); creating a credit union; children carrying out their own research about street life; and forming street theatre groups. The Council has also been instrumental in the formation of the Bal Mazdoor Union (Child Workers' Trade Union).

Problems encountered:

1 Originally, children of each contact point held meetings every fortnight and five representatives from each contact point would come together for the Children's Council each month. However, more of the children wanted to attend the overall meetings, so it became open to all.
2 The venue for the monthly Council meeting is alternated between the contact points. However, it is generally held in 'Old Delhi' (an area encompassing seven of the contact points). For the group of children who work in an area of 'New Delhi' this appears to be an issue, as their level of participation is low. However, they do tend to pass on messages to be taken to the meeting via the street educators.
3 The age range of the children is varied. In some cases, this causes difficulties due to the differing attention span and levels of understanding. For example, debating rules for the credit union was difficult for the children to manage.
4 The street educators remain present during the Children's Council meetings and, on occasion, there has been a tendency for them to take over the agenda. This must be avoided. The children and young people are encouraged to be critical of undue adult interference.
5 Principles of democracy govern meetings but it is questionable whether all the children get an equal say. Some children and groups of children are more vocal and their agenda may sway the meeting.

Main findings of monitoring/research:

The Children's Council itself acts as a mechanism for monitoring the programme orientation and development. The Council meetings ensure that the children actively participate in all issues that are important to them, and they help to ensure that programmes and activities are planned in line with the children's needs and wishes (e.g. a children's rights rally and a kite day). The most commonly discussed issues are: police harassment; non-payment of wages; need for better jobs; wages; education; saving schemes; problems of gambling; drugs. Children have gained confidence in speaking out, some have gone on to participate in conferences, events and press meetings. A street theatre group has developed plays concerning children's issues (e.g. child labour and child sex tourism) which seek to advocate on behalf of children. Thus, it seems that the Children's Council can provide truly child-centred mechanisms which allow children's participation in decision-making to be a central guiding force in any programme or locality development.

Publications/existing documentation:
Alongside their fieldwork Butterflies run DRAC (Documentation, Research and Advocacy Centre), which produces a quarterly child file – *My Name is Today* – which is a compilation of news items about children from various Indian and foreign newspapers, journals and magazines. DRAC produces other advocacy materials on children's rights, including *Taking Education on the Streets*.

4 Young and Proud Group

Location:
Save the Children, Hull.

Start date:
August 1995.

Source of funding:
Joint financing: Health and Social Services, Save the Children and The Warren (a local voluntary organisation).

Number and type of staff:
Four workers (two paid, one volunteer, one student placement).

Number and ages of children and young people:
More than 80 young people, aged 9-20 years. Average age is 14.

Target group:
Young people 'in need' (as identified by The Children Act), particularly those 'at risk', i.e. living on the street, using drugs, in trouble with the police, running away from home or in local authority care.

Role of adults:
To provide information, listen to individual and group views, build trusting relationships with and between the young people, and facilitate problem solving.

Other agencies involved:
Social services (residential and foster care, Youth Court service, local neighbourhood childcare teams); police.

Aims of project/service provided:

1 To provide a safe environment for young people at risk to meet each other and staff. This is achieved by:
- regularly revising ground rules of the YAP group with the young people who attend;
- encouraging group ownership of the YAP ground rules and applying them as consistently as possible;
- ensuring that all new YAP members are informed of the ground rules and the Risk Assessment Procedures on their first night;
- resolving any friction and difficult situations that arise during the YAP group meetings as early as possible, using constructive conflict resolution skills;
- communicating relevant issues, incidents or information through staff and young people during and after the YAP group;
- honesty and openness from the staff about their actions and feelings during the YAP group, thus encouraging the young people to do the same.

2 To work with individual young people at risk on current issues in their lives in order to find resolutions which are in the young person's best interests and also protect any young person at risk from significant harm. This is achieved by:
- building up trusting relationships with young people in the YAP group, based on honesty and openness;
- giving young people information about rights and services appropriate to their situation;
- discussing with young people possible ways of resolving the situations they choose to talk about, including what the young person would most like to see happen.

3 To provide a range of leisure, informal educational activities and support which are relevant and accessible to the young people. This is achieved by:
  - regular consultation with those attending the groups about the events they would like to have;
  - the staff team picking up on the current issues affecting young people in the group and using these to plan informal education workshops;
  - planning events such as workshops, trips out etc., and involving/ supporting any young people who wish to take some responsibility for organising them;
  - ensuring that informal educational workshops are fun, flexible to needs and build upon existing knowledge, skills and experiences.

4 To enable young people's collective voices to be heard by appropriate service providers. This is achieved by:
  - providing opportunities during the YAP group time for young people to discuss shared or similar experiences;
  - providing clear and realistic information to young people about the limits to their involvement, including statutory responsibilities of service providers, limited resources available etc.;
  - working with young people to find opportunities for them to inform relevant service providers about shared issues of concern and suggestions for change.

5 To involve the young people in recruitment of YAP group workers.

Outcomes/benefits for children and young people:
1 The group provides a weekly space for young people to meet each other and workers, and, if they wish, to discuss concerns and incidents.
2 It is still too early to provide hard information about real outcomes, but the project hopes that the benefits of providing a safe place, someone to talk to and listen, as well as a free meal, will become clearer over time.

Problems encountered:
1 Group work, in the traditional sense, is difficult due to the chaotic, transient nature of the children's lives.
2 Most of the children and young people who attend YAP are in constant crisis and live from day to day. YAP must respond to that, and this need often makes it difficult to do more developmental participation work.

Main findings of monitoring/research:
1 School refusal and exclusion is a major trigger to being 'at risk'.
2 Almost all the children and young people participating in YAP have a history of being 'looked after', but most are at home now. However, they still face significant risk and it seems that the social services' response while they were 'accommodated' has failed to get to the root of the problem.
3 Young people may know about some of their rights, but it is much more difficult for them actually to assess services and to feel that they can *do* something to feel more in control of their lives.

5 Circus Eruption

Location:
Swansea.

Start date:
January 1992.

Source of funding:
Foundation for Sports and Arts.

Number and type of staff:
One part-time development worker; one student placement; 20 volunteers; specialist input brought in on an irregular basis, e.g. skill development, theatre director for shows.

Number and age of children and young people:
Young people of 11-19 years. About 40 are involved at any one time.

Target group:
Young people from Swansea who are interested in circus and performance, at least a third of whom have special needs. They must be willing to learn together and support each other in developing skills, and eventually performing shows. Strong emphasis is placed on safety, commitment, mutuality and developing everyone's abilities.

Role of adults:
Support the development of the group; support the individuals in skill and performance development; support activities including parades, shows and festivals; basic back-up and administration; maintaining an adequate pool of volunteers; helping the young people run the circus; counselling and individual support.

Other agencies involved:
The project is co-managed by Playright, a voluntary play promotion organisation, and the local Council for Voluntary Service.

Aims of project/service provided:
General aims:
1 To run a community-based 'new circus' (one that is committed to sharing of skills, with no animals involved).
2 To provide an opportunity for young people of all abilities and disabilities to work together.
3 To develop the potential for all participants in Eruption.
4 To have a good time.
5 To increase awareness of integration and celebrate differences.

Specific service:
The young people elect six to eight delegates who meet with the volunteers' team on a regular basis. At these meetings, the development of the group is planned, day-to-day and crisis management is undertaken, and major decisions are taken, e.g. priorities and commitments. The delegates have weekly meetings with small groups of young people, and sometimes with the whole circus, to make collective decisions.

Outcomes/benefits for children and young people:
1 The young people own and control the project.
2 Young people play an active part in finding solutions to problems and sometimes specifically exclude adults from this process.
3 Young people agree rules and then 'police' them themselves.

4 Young people are used to running meetings and making informed decisions. Several have gone on to be on the board of the National Association of Youth Circus.

Problems encountered:
1 Getting adequate funding to buy equipment.
2 Finding enough volunteers to support the young people safely and who will give the necessary commitment to shows.
3 The span of ages (11-19) means there are problems with alcohol and tobacco.
4 Setting up and adhering to rules of behaviour for people of mixed abilities.
5 Lack of provision for people with special needs at 18+ means that they do not want to leave Eruption when they reach the age limit.

Main findings of monitoring/research:
Integrated Circus works. It is an excellent vehicle for young people to help young people develop and work together. Young people act as advocates for integration, they gain experiences completely outside the norm, and both their performances and the culture of the organisation is about ability rather than disability.

Publications/existing documentation:
Annual reports available from INTERPLAY.

6 It's My Life

Location:
Children's Rights Service, Chelmsford, Essex.

Start date:
April 1995.

Source of funding:
Essex Social Services Department; one-off charitable donations for specific events.

Number and type of staff:
One, plus residential social worker, and social work and family carer volunteers.

Number and ages of children and young people:
Approximately 45 children and young people aged 10-23 years.

Target group:
Children and young people receiving help from social services and their friends; children being looked after and in need.

Role of adults:
Initially to set up the project; now adults work as facilitators and provide support to the projects initiated by young people.

Other agencies involved:
Schools for young people with learning difficulties; the youth service; independent voluntary arts organisation working with disadvantaged and disabled people.

Aims of project/service provided:
1 Encourage learning development – rights advocacy and participation in social care issues.
2 Set up a standing conference of young people who care about social care issues.
3 Provide peer education.
4 Provide consultation service and training.
5 Promote social contact and fund by developing arts/drama communication skills for young people who are looked after in or leaving care.

Outcomes/benefits for children and young people:
1 Learning development – work done as part of the group can be used for GNVQ core skills.
2 Young people influence change in culture of the local authority's working practices.
3 There has been a growth in self-esteem, responsibility, in making new relationships and networking.
4 The young people have had fun.

Problems encountered:
1 The project covers a large geographical area and the young people are dependent on adults for transport.
2 There have been difficulties in raising the core funding to assist in the independence of the project.
3 More adult support is required to assist young people in moving forward and achieving complete autonomy.

Main findings of monitoring/research:
1 The welfare of children vs the right to self determination is a difficult issue for adults to assimilate.
2 Once they are engaged in far-reaching participation, young people demonstrate that adults have much to learn about their ability to make decisions.
3 Peer education is very effective.

Publications/existing documentation:
1 Videos: a signed and subtitled video for young people; a training video for social services; and a training video for 'Looking After Children', which is part of a DoH initiative.
2 Report of children's rights awayday.

7 Community Youth Development

Location:
Niddrie Adventure Playground, Edinburgh.

Start date:
August 1995.

Source of funding:
Tudor Trust.

Number and type of staff:
One full time; one sessional.

Number and ages of children and young people:
Approximately 15 young people, aged 16-21 years. Two groups run concurrently to fulfil the CYD's two main aims – the Open Group and the Focus Group. Each group operates with a core group of 8-10 individuals, augmented by three to four non-regular attenders. Each group meets collectively at least once a week for two hours, with additional sessions arranged as required. On average, a further four to eight hours per week is spent supporting group members on group-related tasks, and a further four to six hours supporting individuals to deal with personal issues.

Target group:
Young marginalised adults.

Role of adults:
Facilitators.

Other agencies involved:
Community Education, social workers and many smaller voluntary agencies.

Aims of project/service provided:
1 Open Group: To provide opportunities for local young people to participate in groups which assist them to take action designed to improve their life opportunities in general. Some of the activities in which this group is involved include:
   - setting up and running a local primary school football team;
   - bronze medallion training (lifesaving and personal survival);
   - first aid training;
   - helping a local organisation tidy up and landscape its grounds;
   - organise a local football tournament;
   - identifying and taking part in externally run training, e.g. Housing and Benefits.
2 Focus Group: To support local young people in achieving the specific goal of establishing a new youth facility in the community which has separate funding and management arrangements.
   Within these two main aims, also to support young people on an individual basis, to enable them to participate fully in the project and resolve issues of personal concern.

Outcomes/benefits for children and young people:
1 The social action approach of the Open Group serves to improve the general quality of life of the young people involved.
2 The Open Group also develops transferable life skills rather than those which are simply used for accreditation under a specific scheme.
3 Focus Group members are actively involved in the steering and management committees for local development.

4 Focus Group members also take part in appropriate training which enables them to become service providers as well as service users in e.g. youth work, peer education, health and safety, and counselling.

Problems encountered:
Accessing the relevant age group, retaining the interest of those involved and establishing positive expectations among that group.

8 Chailey Young People's Group

Location:
Chailey, East Sussex.

Start date:
Funded from November 1994; fully operational April 1995.

Source of funding:
South Downs NHS Trust.

Number and type of staff:
One children and young people's advocate (independent of Chailey Heritage services) assisted by Chailey Heritage staff.

Number and ages of children and young people:
Approximately 8-10 children/young people, aged 12-18 years.

Target group:
Children and young people with severe, complex and multiple physical disabilities who use Chailey Heritage services (residential; school; out-patients).

Role of adults:
To facilitate CYPG with staff support; to advocate on behalf of group members; to operate communication systems as most CYPG members do not have spoken communication.

Aims of project/service provided:
To enable young people who use Chailey Heritage services to meet together, communicate with each other, share points of view, express ideas and help solve problems (young people's own words). The young people initiated the idea for this group, they planned it and decided on its aims. They have been involved all the way through and have also attended an advocacy conference to inform others of this group and its purpose.

Outcomes/benefits for children and young people:
Young people have used CYPG in several ways:
- as a safe place to bring problems which may be dealt with within the group or pursued by the advocate;
- as a place to communicate with each other about anything;
- as a means of empowerment through sharing personal experiences and peer support.

Problems encountered:
There were no significant problems, as the young people initiated the whole project themselves.

Main findings of monitoring/research:
With increasing support from Chailey staff (e.g. communication and transport) the group has had consistent attendance. The young people are very committed and use the group well. The group is used:
- to discuss and pursue relationship difficulties with staff and teachers;
- for practical issues;
- to obtain advice;
- for group complaints e.g. to companies or organisations about their provisions for disabled users;
- to share experiences of disability;
- to promote their views so that they are heard.

Publications/existing documentation:
1 Quarterly reports.
2 Leaflet designed and written by CYPG members (see Figure 7.1).

Figure 7.1

9 The Children's Planning Initiative

Location:
Salford.

Start date:
1991.

Source of funding:
The Children's Society and local authority partners.

Number and type of staff:
Two professionals with part-time administrator and assistant.

Number and ages of children and young people:
Approximately 30 children and young people aged 0-20.

Target group:
Children and young people in the 'looked after' system.

Role of adults:
To provide independent coordination and administration of planning processes around each young person. Coordinators of planning groups are charged with implementing a set of key principles (e.g. centrality of child's wishes and feelings) in planning rather than operating to set procedures. They must convene planning meetings and facilitate these in accordance with the principles of the project.

Other agencies involved:
The project works in partnership with local authorities who look after children.

Aims of project/service provided:
To implement Articles 3 and 12 of the UN Convention on the Rights of the Child alongside key principles contained in the Children Act (1989), notably those relating to the need for young people, their families and professionals to work in partnership to make decisions. To do this the Children's Planning Initiative not only ensures a hearing for children within existing systems, it develops new flexible processes within which partnership can become a reality for young people and non-professionals. This is achieved by constructing unique planning groups around each child, each one operating in a way that is meaningful to the child concerned (e.g. by attending to membership, process, minutes etc. from the young person's point of view).

Outcomes/benefits for children and young people:
A forum is created and independently coordinated in which a young person is able to speak openly and experience being taken seriously. A forum is created whereby young people can draw on adults as a resource and can increasingly take on responsibility for their own lives. Decisions are not professionalised or bureaucratised; they are brought closer to the child or young person concerned.

Problems encountered:
Staff in the 'looked after' system understandably feel threatened by the involvement of independent people, particularly as, in other contexts, such independents often arrive at times of conflict. The aim of the Children's Planning Initiative is to work in partnership with the other adults involved, rather than to work against them.

Main findings of monitoring/research:
The project has seen the successful creation of planning partnerships,

and success in integrating young people and professionals into planning processes in cases where they have not taken part in the past. An early small-scale internal statistical survey found that the approach used can be highly effective in getting things done, while a recent partnership with a local authority children's home has seen considerable impact on existing systems within social services. It has played an important part in the development of more positive, trusting relationships within the home, as staff and young people have worked with the project to implement the principles.

There have been many examples of young people expressing wishes that have gone against earlier decisions, or challenging agencies' policies within CPI planning groups. These have resulted in a change of decision, or even a new policy. The creativity of planning groups has often resulted in agencies trying out new ideas with regard to the young people they look after.

Publications/existing documentation:
An external researcher's report from January 1994 is available from the project through the Children's Society in Salford.

10 MINDSCAPE

Location:
Cambuslang, South Lanarkshire.

Start date:
First discussions, April 1992; constituted as independent group, July 1995.

Source of funding:
Volunteer expenses from the Sparky Project (SCF); occasional charges to user group.

Number and type of staff:
Support provided by project leader, Sparky Project.

Number and ages of children and young people:
Four young people aged 17-20 years (the members) organise the adventure games. These are made available to children of all ages.

Target group:
The adventure games are devised for children and young people in and around Glasgow, both disabled and non-disabled. They raise awareness of disability rights.

Role of adult:
1 Advisory – the group was initiated and is directed by the members (see Figure 1.1). They chose the level of adult involvement, which was 'Adults are available but do not take charge'.
2 Provides some workshops on basic organisational skills, such as planning, costing and publicity.
3 Occasionally offers planning or monitoring exercises, but do not participate.

Other agencies involved:
None.

Aims of project/service provided:
MINDSCAPE members devise, organise and lead 'inclusive' adventure games which are accessible to people with a range of impairments and aimed at raising awareness of disability rights. These games are free, or free at the point of delivery, and have been arranged for a variety of organisations and client groups.

Outcomes/benefits for children and young people:
Confidence and skill levels have been raised for the four members. For the children who attend adventure games, there is:
- more confidence among disabled and non-disabled young people about playing with each other;
- less isolation for disabled children;
- encouragement for non-disabled children to make themselves more available to disabled children.

Problems encountered:
1 Lack of funds for travel and equipment costs.
2 Failure to achieve independent funding.
3 Limited contact between worker and members.

Main findings of monitoring/research:
No formal evaluation has been undertaken of the group. Evaluations of individual games by client organisations have all been very favourable.

11 Sick of Zero Status: European Hearing on Youth

Location:
Swansea.

Start date:
Planning started in November 1995; Hearing held in February 1996.

Source of funding:
Socialist Group of MEPs.

Number and type of staff:
One facilitator for planning and preparation; support from four facilitators on Youth Hearing Day; additional support from three youth workers; one report writer.

Number and ages of children and young people:
Planning group was 15 young people aged 17-22; Hearing attended by over 100 participants aged 16-60.

Target group:
Young unemployed people who wished to voice an opinion to politicians, policy-makers, local employers, etc. People from West and Mid Glamorgan.

Role of adults:
Facilitator to enable young people to crystallise their ideas as they set up, ran and evaluated the Youth Hearing; youth workers to provide administration back-up; more facilitators to help young people run the hearing on the day; report writer to provide objective overview.

Other agencies involved:
Youth Services of West and Mid Glamorgan; Bridgend YMCA.

Aims of project/service provided:
General aims:
1 To give young people the opportunity to have their voice heard and to express their opinions on youth unemployment.
2 To ensure that the young people owned, controlled and led the planning and the event itself.
3 To help young people develop the skills and confidence to run workshops for politicians, officers, employers and other young people.
4 To reach as many young people as possible and give them a positive atmosphere in which to speak.

Services provided:
1 The planning group of young people planned and facilitated a youth hearing consisting of a keynote speaker, a series of workshops, a thought-provoking lunch, and plenary sessions to decide the outcome of the hearing and recommendations.
2 The planning group had six meetings between November 1995 and February 1996 during which they received training to give them the confidence to run sessions and chair the plenary sessions.

Outcomes/benefits for children and young people:
1 A great sense of achievement and personal development by the planning group.
2 A more positive attitude among members of the planning group and hearing participants.
3 An exciting and challenging day attended by over 100 people.
4 Lots of media attention – the young people were offered the chance to make two TV documentaries.

5 The articulation of young people's demands for change in youth employment and training.

Problems encountered:
1 Lack of confidence among members of the planning group.
2 Scepticism of professionals that young people could manage the event.
3 Difficulty in distributing information due to political message (it had a red rose on it!).
4 Difficulty in reaching young people.
5 Problems with getting adequate reliable transport to get young people to the event.
6 Unwillingness of politicians and other professionals to listen to young people.

Bibliography and further reading

The following publications provide more background and ideas for encouraging participation. They deal with various area of policy and practice, and many include practical activities. Some of them are referred to in the text. All Save the Children publications can be obtained from: Save the Children, c/o NBN Plymbridge, Estover Road, Plymouth, PL6 7PY. Tel: 01752 202301; email: orders@plymbridge.com

Beresford, B. and Croft, S. (1993) *Citizen Involvement – A Practical Guide for Change*, Macmillan, Basingstoke

British Association for Community Child Health/Children's Rights Office (1995) *Child Health Rights: Implementing the UN Convention on the Rights of the Child Within the Health Service – A Practitioner's Guide*, BACCH/CRO, London

British Youth Council, *Local Action*, British Youth Council, London

Chauhan, V., Oldfield, C. and White, P. (1990) *The Youth Action Book*, National Youth Action Bureau (now National Youth Agency), Leicester

Children's Rights Development Unit (1994) *UK Agenda for Children*, CRDU, London

Croft, S. and Beresford, B. (1993) *Getting Involved*, Open Service Project, London

Devon Youth Council (1994) *Devon Youth Council Pack*, Devon Youth Council, Exeter

Dickson, A. (1982) *A Woman in Your Own Right – Assertiveness and You*, Quartet Books, London

Duke, L. et al. (1991) *Face to Face: A Practitioner's Manual on Personal Development Work with Young People in Northern Ireland*, Save the Children, London

Fountain, S. (1993) *It's Only Right*, UNICEF, London

Graham, J. (1985) *The Youth Club's Participation Starter Kit*, Youth Clubs UK, London

Graham, J. (1992) *Taking the Wraps off Participation*, Youth Clubs UK, London

Greenaway, R. (1990) *Young People (II): More Than Activities*, Save the Children, London

Hart, R. (1992) *Child's Participation: From Tokenism to Citizenship*, UNICEF International Child Development Centre, London

Kealy, L. (1993) *Consulting with Young People on Sealand Manor, Clwyd*, Wales Youth Agency and Wales Youth Forum, Caerphilly

Keenan, E. (1988) 'Social action groupwork as negotiation: contradictions in the process of empowerment', *Groupwork*, 1, 3, 229-38

Lifechance (1994) *Lifechance Project Annual Report 1993/4*, Save the Children, London

Meynell (1993) *Meynell Games On . . . Parachute Play*, Meynell Games Publications, London

Price, L. (1993a) *Introduction to Participation and Involvement*, Night Shift Enterprises, Abergavenny

Price, L. (1993b) *Starting a Members' Group*, Night Shift Enterprises, Abergavenny

Price, L. (1996) *Senior Member Training – Involving Young People 16+*, vol. 1, Night Shift Enterprises, Abergavenny

Price, L. (1996) *Senior Member Training – Involving Young People 16+*, vol. 2, Night Shift Enterprises, Abergavenny

Rieser, R. and Mason, M. (1992) *Disability Equality in the Classroom: A Human Rights Issue*, Disability Equality in Education, 78 Mildmay Grove, London N1 4PJ. Price £15

Save the Children (2000) *Children as Partners in Planning: A training resource to support consultation with children*, Save the Children, London

Save the Children (2003) *Never too young: How children can take responsibility and make decisions – A Handbook for Early Years Workers*, Save the Children, London

Sharp, S. and Smith, P. K. (1991) 'Bullying in Schools: the DES Sheffield Bullying Project', *Early Child Development and Care*, vol. 77

Shepherd, C. and Treseder, P. (2002) *Participation – Spice it Up! Practical tools for engaging children and young people in planning and consultations*, Save the Children/Dynamix, London

Smith, M. (1981) *Organise: A Guide to Practical Politics for Youth and Community Groups*, Youth Clubs UK, London

Smith, M. (1981) *Participation: Creators Not Consumers, Rediscovering Social Education*, Youth Clubs UK, London

Who Cares Trust & National Consumer Council (1993) *Not just a name: the views of young people in foster and residential care*, Who Cares Trust and NCC, London

Wilcox, D. (1994) *The Guide to Effective Participation*, Partnership Books, Brighton

Williamson, H. (ed.) (1995) *Social Action for Young People – Accounts of SCF Youth Work Practice*, Save the Children, London

Youth Council for Northern Ireland (1993) *Participation – Youth Work Curriculum Guidelines*, YCNI, Belfast

Free leaflets
Llanedeyrn Report, Wales Youth Agency, Caerphilly
Playing Fair: a parents' guide to tackling discrimination, National Early Years Network, London
Promoting Participation, Save the Children, London
Spotlight (four issues per year), Save the Children, London
What Would You Do If You Were . . ., Save the Children, London

Parachute games
Parachute games and training in parachute play are run throughout the UK by DYNAMIX Ltd, 14 Montpellier Terrace, Mount Pleasant, Swansea SA1 6JW. Tel: 01792 466231. Playchutes can be obtained from SeamStress, 14 Spring Street, Chipping Norton, Oxfordshire OX7 5NN. Tel: 01608 642651. SeamStress produce a booklet, *Parachute Games*, which costs £3.00. Meynell Games (0181-446-5551) also produces a book, called *Meynell Games On . . . Parachute Play*, price £20.